God and Cancer:

Finding Hope in the Midst of Life's Trials

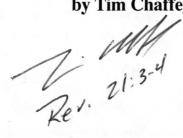

by Tim Chaffey

Rev. 21:3-4

Table of Contents

Acknowledgements

I would like to say a huge "Thank You" to the following people that helped make this book a reality:

- Pastor and English teacher Glenn Andes for your advice and finding time to proofread the manuscript.
- Dr. Tommy Mitchell for your encouragement and your insights contained in Appendix B.
- The amazing team of doctors and nurses at St. Mary's Hospital in Green Bay and all the other medical personnel that treated me during my illness. You saved my life.
- All the faithful believers that kept me in prayer during my battle with leukemia.
- My friends and family members for keeping me company in the hospital, whether in person or by phone calls, emails, or cards.
- My lovely wife Casey. You stood by me and were a rock every step of the way. You are so much better

than I deserve, and I love you more than words can say.

- Most importantly, my Lord and Savior Jesus Christ. You walked with me, and at times, carried me through the valley of the shadow of death. You paid the penalty that I deserve, have given me eternal life, and I am privileged to give you my life in return.

Preface

"You have cancer." These three words are some of the most dreadful words anyone could ever hear. Millions of people have lost their lives due to this awful disease, so hearing these words from one's doctor will strike fear into the bravest of souls. These words are almost identical to the words I heard from my doctor on July 12, 2006.

Actually, the words I heard on that fateful day were, "You have leukemia." At the time, I was 32 years old and in pretty good physical shape. I never thought I would have to worry about cancer until I was at least in my forties, and since my family has not had much of a history with the disease, I felt pretty safe. I was wrong.

In a moment my world was turned upside down. Everything was going well in my life. Everyone in my family was healthy, and we had been spending a great deal of quality time together over the summer. My career was going well as I was preparing to start teaching Bible classes again after a year in the science department. I believed that God had been preparing me for this moment, and I was excited about the opportunity to start teaching the subject closest to my heart. My speaking ministry was starting to pick up, and I had just finished the rough draft to my first book.[1]

Everything was great – at least that's what I thought at the time. Little did I know that I was dying on the inside. Those three words changed my life forever. I spent the next month in the hospital fighting for my life and several more months recovering from the side effects of four rounds of chemotherapy. In fact, as I type this sentence, I am still feeling some of the effects of the treatments – more than four months after my last dose of chemo.

Thankfully, I am now a cancer survivor. I am one of the "lucky" ones, if there is such a thing. A large percentage of people who hear those words will never get a second chance at life. I believe people should use the knowledge they gain from their experiences to help others who are going through similar situations. This is my primary purpose for writing this book. I want to provide hope and comfort for people who are dealing with a cancer diagnosis or have a loved one who has been diagnosed.

I am also a Bible-believing Christian. I believe that God has a purpose and plan for everyone in this world. When tragedy strikes, it is difficult for many people to believe that a loving God is in control of this world. My hope is that by the time you have finished reading this book, you will be able to see that the existence of cancer and other horrible things in this world do not negate the existence of God nor should they cause one to despair and lose hope.

Whether you agree with my views of God and the Bible or not, the practical advice given at the end of each chapter may prove beneficial. I simply want you to understand where I am coming from. When I use examples from the Bible, it is important for you to know that I believe these were actual people who went through real struggles in real history. To help convince you of the historicity and inspiration of Scripture is beyond the focus of this book; however the final section of this book will cover some basic material in this area for those who might have questions.

That being said, I invite you to go on a journey with me. This journey started in the summer of 2006, is continuing as I write this book, and will continue for the rest of my life. May you be encouraged and find hope in the following pages.

Each chapter in the first section of this book will highlight a different segment of my ordeal with leukemia. It will begin with the initial symptoms, move on through the diagnosis and treatment, and conclude with my recovery. Through each step of the way, I will attempt to provide hope to those going through similar difficulties by offering practical advice and theological insights. One thing that I have always believed, and had firmly reinforced during my battle, was that having the right attitude goes a long way in getting through tough situations.

Some medical terms are printed in bold type the first time they appear. There is a glossary at the end of the book to define these terms.

Part One:

My Story

Introduction:
Something's Wrong

The summer months are usually a wonderful time for a teacher. The summer of 2006 was shaping up to be another summer of reading, research, recreation, and relaxation. I enjoyed getting up in the morning while it was still cool and going for my daily walk. This gave me a chance to plan my day and to spend time thinking about whatever was on my mind.

In the last week of June, I began to notice that something was askew. My normal walk was a three-mile route and if I was feeling especially ambitious, I would go further. The first sign of trouble was that it seemed harder and harder to make it through the entire route. At first, I didn't think much of this as I simply chalked it up to being out of shape. I told myself that all I had to do was to keep pushing myself and soon it would get easier.

One day near the end of June, I woke up with the worst leg cramps I have ever had. I could not think of anything that I had done to aggravate my legs, but it still never crossed my mind that something serious was going on.

At about this same time, I noticed dozens of tiny purple spots on the top of my feet. Not knowing what to make of these, my wife and I did what everyone does these days – we searched the internet to find out what was causing these spots. Our "expert" conclusion was that they were simply a result of a heat rash. After all, one's feet can get pretty warm during a long walk in the summer. I would later discover that we were way off on our diagnosis.

Being as stubborn as the next guy, I never thought about going to the doctor to see if something else was causing these symptoms. So I decided to press on. As a former college athlete, I believe in the mantra, "no pain, no gain." If I was going to get myself in shape I was going to push right through the tough times. My legs were still cramped up, but I decided that I needed to keep exercising and they would loosen up.

In the first week of July, we packed up the van and headed to the Cincinnati, Ohio area for a conference. I remember the trouble that I had walking to the various sessions because of the soreness in my legs. We were staying with a friend in the area who happened to be my school's Physical Education teacher. I talked to him about the cramping in my legs and we concluded that it must have occurred during stretching one night. I remembered sitting in the "butterfly stretch" position for a long time the night before I first noticed the cramping. I must have stayed in the position too long. This put my mind at ease and I had renewed resolve to push through the pain.

During the following week, I continued with my daily walks; however, I was starting to get more concerned. It was becoming increasingly difficult to make it through the entire walk, and every time I was going uphill, I got extremely winded.

Following church that weekend, I spoke with a close family friend. She suggested that I might be dehydrated. That conclusion had not occurred to me, and the symptoms seemed to line up (except for the purple spots). Dehydration also made sense because I had been drinking a lot of iced tea at the time and caffeinated beverages do not help much in hydrating the body. I decided to stop drinking the tea and start drinking large quantities of water.

The next day was Monday, July 10th. I went for my morning walk and had to turn around about halfway through the route. When I stopped and turned, I nearly passed out. Now I was very concerned. I was afraid that I might not be able to make it back to the house. I did make it back and after taking a few minutes to catch my breath, I jumped in the car and drove to the nearest store to load up on sports drinks. If I was dehydrated, I was going to put a quick stop to it. I drank more than ten cups of sports drink that day.

Another symptom began to rear its ugly head that day. My gums began to bleed after brushing my teeth. My gums have bled before, so I was not overly concerned until I awoke the next morning and noticed that they were still bleeding.

I thought that I would be fine to go for my walk that day. After all, I drank so much Gatorade that there was no way for me to be dehydrated anymore. Once again, I was wrong. I had barely left my driveway on Tuesday morning when fatigue and shortness of breath forced me to return home. I guzzled several more quarts of sports drink.

That night, I stayed home with the kids while my wife went to a movie with some friends. Around 7:00 I started to feel pretty ill and decided to lie down and throw in a movie for the kids to watch with me. I made it through the night and woke up feeling much better.

It was now Wednesday, July 12th, a day that will live in infamy for my family. I laced up my shoes to go for another walk. This time, I had forgotten something upstairs so I decided to go get it before the walk. By the time I had reached the top of the stairs, I was so winded that I had to sit down to catch my breath. This was the last straw.

I called the nurse and explained the symptoms to her. She thought it would be a good idea to come in to see if they could figure out what was going on. I figured that I would go in for a few hours and get a couple of IV bags of fluid pumped into me before getting the "all clear." Boy, was I ever naïve.

Chapter One:

The Diagnosis

"The LORD gave and the LORD has taken away;
may the name of the LORD be praised."
- Job 1: 21b

The Local Clinic

On the morning of July 12th, I drove to the local clinic expecting to be treated for dehydration. I talked with my doctor about my symptoms and he ordered a blood test. After waiting for nearly an hour I met with my doctor again.

He showed me the results of the blood work and told me that he was very concerned. My white blood cell count should have been between 3,000 and 5,000. Instead, it had skyrocketed to over 60,000. This meant that my body was unsuccessfully trying to fight off an infection of some sort.

While my white blood cell count was extremely high, my **platelet** count was extremely low. A normal platelet count runs between 140 and 440. Mine were under 20. This was the reason for all of the little reddish-purple spots on my feet that I attributed to a heat rash. They were, in fact, **petechiae**, which are a sure sign of a low platelet count.

My doctor then told me some words that I never thought I would hear. He said, "I'm very concerned about these numbers. They indicate that you have some type of viral infection or a blood cancer. You need to go to Madison right away."

He took me out to the appointment desk and handed the woman behind the desk a note to make an emergency appointment for me in Madison. On the card, he had written the word "**thrombocytopenia**." I wrote it down so that I could look it up if given the chance.

The woman told me that the doctor in Madison could see me at 11:45. The problem was that Madison was more than an hour away and it was already 11:00. She realized that I would never make it and told me that the doctor in Madison would see me as soon as I arrived.

On the way out of the clinic, I phoned my wife, Casey, and told her that she needed to get the babysitter over right away because we had to go to Madison. I told her what the doctor had said, and, as the eternal optimist that I am, I told her that I was sure it was just a viral infection.

The gravity of the situation did not really hit me until I got off the phone with Casey and got in my car. For the first time, it crossed my mind that I might actually have cancer. As I pulled away from the clinic, the song playing in my car stereo was all about how God was able to make me stand no matter what trouble may come. I cried during most of the fifteen minute drive home and tried to compose myself before reaching the house.

Upon arriving at home I hugged my wife and kids and impatiently waited for the babysitter to arrive. As we waited, I decided to look up "thrombocytopenia" on the internet. My heart sank as I instantly saw the word "leukemia" as one of the major causes of this symptom. I closed the webpage before Casey could see it because I did not want her to think about it during the drive to Madison.

The sitter arrived about ten minutes after me. I hugged my kids again and headed out with my wife. Little did I know that I would not see the house again for well over a month. The drive to Madison seemed to last for hours as we sat quietly fearing the worst. We prayed and prayed that it was just a viral infection that could be treated, but after seeing "leukemia" on the internet, my optimism was quickly fading.

Madison, WI – The Diagnosis

We arrived at the clinic in Madison around one o'clock in the afternoon, and I had some more blood tests. My earlier test results had already been sent to Madison so the doctor was familiar with my case. Before the results came in, he was asking me questions about my family's history with cancer and whether or not I had any siblings. I was just focused on answering the questions and hoping against hope that it was a viral infection, so it did not really occur to me that he already knew it was cancer. When he left the room, my wife looked at me with tears running down her face and told me that it was cancer. She said she knew based on the questions he was asking. That's when it finally hit me. I had cancer.

The doctor returned a few minutes later with the results of the blood tests. He looked me right in the eyes and said, "You've got leukemia." My first response was to ask if he was positive it wasn't a viral infection. He told me that he was absolutely sure that it was leukemia.

I was then informed about the severity of my situation. I was extremely sick and was soon hurried into another room where I would receive the first of many bone marrow biopsies. The procedure only lasts a few minutes but is quite painful during that time. The pain from this first biopsy barely bothered me because my mind was still reeling from the diagnosis.

A few minutes later, as I sat and talked to the nurse, I began to realize what I was up against. I asked her how long it would be before I could return to teaching, and she told me that I would not be teaching at all during the upcoming school year. That was the third most difficult thing I had endured that day. The first was the actual diagnosis and the second was coming up.

The doctor told us to go out for lunch and return two hours later, and then he would have some more information about my diagnosis. He also told me that I needed to be very careful not to bump into anything, trip, or do anything else that might cause me to bleed. He warned me that if I started bleeding it would not stop because of the low platelet count.

We drove to a nearby fast food restaurant and ordered very little. Neither of us could eat much so we sat down and started calling people with the bad news. Within an hour of being diagnosed, I was added to prayer lists all over the country. After calling several friends, family members, and co-workers, we returned to the hospital.

We sat in the waiting room and could barely compose ourselves during what seemed like "millions of years." As we sat there, two people from the community came in to donate a signed and framed Lance Armstrong jersey. For those unfamiliar with Lance Armstrong, he achieved one of the most amazing athletic feats in history. He won the Tour de France cycling race an incredible seven consecutive years. This means he was at the very top of his sport for seven years. Not many can compare to that. What makes this even more impressive is that he won his first Tour just three years after being diagnosed with testicular cancer. He endured extensive chemotherapy and went through brain and testicular surgeries. The sight of his jersey was a great encouragement to me. If he could become a cancer survivor, so could I.

We were called back to the examining room and this time received the first good news of the day. The doctor had examined my blood under the microscope and thought that my type of leukemia was acute promyelocytic leukemia, also known as M3 leukemia or APL for short. He said that this kind of leukemia had the highest remission success rate. I asked him if it was over fifty percent and he said, "It's the only one that is."

He then informed me that I needed to be admitted to the hospital immediately so they could begin the induction stage of treatment. He left the room so that we could discuss things for a while.

Up until this point, I had not been able to get a hold of my parents, and I wanted to talk to them first. I had tried calling my father but did not get an answer. I did not know that my dad had just purchased a new cell phone and given his old one to my mom. When I tried the number again, my mom answered. I did not want to be the one to break the news to her. I was hoping that I could talk to my dad and he would be the one to tell her. Now, since she answered the phone, I had to tell her. That was the second toughest thing I went through that day.

Soon after that, my dad called me. He had been driving through Pennsylvania on business when he got the news. He and I agreed that it would be best if I could be treated in Green Bay so that we could be close to family. If we stayed in Madison, my wife and kids would be a little more than an hour away. If we went to Green Bay, they could stay with my parents and be less than fifteen minutes away from the hospital.

When the doctor returned to the room, we told him that we wanted to go to Green Bay for treatment. He was not in favor of the idea but reluctantly agreed to it. Again he cautioned me about doing anything that might cause bleeding. He gave us the name of an **oncologist** in Green Bay with whom he had gone to medical school many years earlier.

We left the clinic and called some family friends to see if they would be willing to drive to our house, pack up our kids and some belongings, and meet us in Madison. Thankfully, they were willing to help us out by doing this.

As we waited for what seemed like days, we called several more people that we had not had a chance to tell before. It was tough to watch my wife try to tell her sister about the diagnosis. It took a long time before she could even say the words, "Tim has leukemia." I tried to make arrangements with the Green Bay hospital to allow me to check in that night but they decided to have me wait until the following morning.

Our friends finally arrived with our children and belongings. We hugged, said our goodbyes, and headed for Green Bay. The three-hour drive to Green Bay was filled with more phone calls and more tears.

I did receive some more good news during that evening. I had thought the success rate for my type of leukemia was right around 50% based on my doctor's comments. My cousin called me while we were waiting for our kids and told me that he saw reports of the success rates being around 70% and possibly higher for younger, healthier patients. Finally, during the drive, I received another phone call. It just so happened (call it luck or coincidence if you like, but I prefer to call it Providence) that when my brother-in-law, also a doctor, heard about my diagnosis, he happened to be standing next to an oncologist. The oncologist told him that the success rate for M3 leukemia was around 90% and again, a little higher for younger, healthier patients. The high success rate is also in part due to some new drugs that had recently been developed. Obviously, this provided an incredible lift to our spirits.

I like to think of these percentages in terms of my favorite sport, basketball. At first, when I thought I had a 50% chance I was thinking in terms of Shaquille O'Neal shooting a free throw – and that wasn't pretty. When I heard that I had better than 70% chance, I began to think about myself at the free throw line. Finally, when I got the news from my brother-in-law, I thought about Reggie Miller or Dirk Nowitzki, two of the best free throw shooters in history. That helped quite a bit. In my mind, I had gone from a fifty-fifty chance to better than 90 percent in just a matter of hours. Of course, in reality, the 90% was a more accurate figure from the start. It would be difficult to explain how much this news helped us during our first night. We went from thinking we had a 50/50 chance to having an excellent opportunity to win the fight against leukemia.

Green Bay

We arrived at my parents' house in the Green Bay area around eleven o'clock that night. It was great to see my mom after our agonizing phone conversation. I decided to hook up the computer and send out an email to everyone on the Midwest Apologetics[1] mailing list informing them of the diagnosis and to ask for their prayers.

After talking with my mom for a while we decided to try to get some sleep. Instead of sleeping, my wife and I stayed awake almost the entire night hoping and praying that everything would be alright. I slept a total of about two hours that night.

I got up around four in the morning and decided to start a journal on the website that I could add to each day to keep people updated on my situation.[2] This proved to become a valuable tool for us. During the first few days in the hospital, Casey received about ten calls a day in which she answered the same questions over and over again. Once people were informed about the journal, they were able to check out my progress online and Casey could focus on other things. Second, the journal has helped form the basis of this book. We received numerous comments about how encouraged people were when reading the journal that we believed it would be possible to provide comfort to countless others by putting this book together.

As instructed the night before, I called the hospital at 7:30 AM to schedule my appointment for admission. Then, my son and I played catch with a big rubber ball in my parents' family room. As I watched my three year old boy catch and throw, I began to wonder if I would ever have a chance to play catch like so many fathers and sons have done before. My wife took pictures of me sitting with my daughter and then with my son.

It was a strange morning because there was so much uncertainty and nervous tension in the air. Would this be my last visit to my parents' house? Would this be the last time I ever played with my kids? We didn't know. All we could do was face the battle ahead of us with confidence that God was on our side.

A few more family members came over in the morning to watch the kids so that my mom could go to the hospital with my wife and me. I took my last breath of fresh air for nearly a month as we walked into the hospital around 9:00 AM.

Hope in the Midst of Despair

As we had waited in Madison on July 12 for our friends to bring our children to us, I began to think about Job. The

Book of Job is found in the Old Testament in the Bible. It is possibly the oldest book of the Bible and deals with the sufferings of a very godly man named Job. He probably lived around 2000 B.C., near or possibly before the time of Abraham.

Job was a very wealthy man with seven thousand sheep, three thousand camels, and hundreds of other animals. He was blessed with seven sons and three daughters. Job 1: 3 describes him as "the greatest man among all the people of the East."

The Bible tells us that one day, Satan challenged God that if He would stop blessing Job, then Job would curse Him. The Lord told Satan that he could do whatever he wanted to Job as long as he did not lay a hand on Job himself. Job was about to lose nearly everything. Satan's attack cost Job his children, his livestock, his servants, and his wealth – all in one day!

What would Job do? Would he curse God as Satan suggested? Job 1: 20 – 21 records his reaction:

> At this, Job got up and tore his robe and shaved his head. Then he fell to the ground in worship and said: "Naked I came from my mother's womb, and naked I will depart. The LORD gave and the LORD has taken away; may the name of the LORD be praised."

The story does not end there. The second chapter tells us that Satan asked permission to strike Job's health, and God allowed him to do it. Job was struck with painful boils all over his body. As he mourned, he used broken pottery to scrape the boils on his body. Not only was he suffering tremendous emotional turmoil, but now he was enduring horrific physical pain. His wife didn't help the situation much. She told him to "Curse God and die!" (Job 2: 9).[3]

How would Job handle this latest round of attacks? Would he do what Satan claimed? Would he follow his wife's advice? Job replied to his wife, "You speak as one of the foolish women speaks. Shall we indeed accept good from God, and shall we not accept adversity?" Job understood that in a sin-cursed world good things happen to "good people and bad people," and bad things happen to "good people and bad people."[4] He believed that all things were under God's control, and that he did not have the right to turn on God when things got tough.

Thinking about this righteous man's reaction helped me through my struggles. First, I still had my family and my possessions. My life was in serious trouble, but God had given me thirty-two wonderful years of life and nearly a decade (at the time) of marriage to a wife who, thankfully, did not respond in the same manner as Job's wife.

She was always very supportive and was with me every step of the way.

I was thankful for the life I had lived and hoped for an opportunity to see my kids grow older. The worst thing that could happen would be for me to lose the battle with leukemia but, at the same time, I believe that if I died, I would be with my Lord. I also believe that God works all things together for the good of those who love Him (Romans 8: 28).

I had a strong sense that He was not finished with me yet, and that I would be able to use my experiences to bring comfort and hope to others. As I write these words, I have already had the opportunity to give my testimony before several audiences. I have heard from many people that they were blessed through reading my journal or listening to my talk on the subject. As far as I am concerned, that makes the entire battle worthwhile.

You might ask, "Why does God allow horrible things like this to happen to anyone? Why is there so much suffering in the world? If there is a loving God, why does He allow bad things to happen to those who love Him the most?" These are great questions and will be dealt with in the following chapters.

Chapter 2:

The Razor Blade of Life

"What is your life? You are a mist that appears for a little while and then vanishes."
- James 4: 14b

Checking In

R enewed confidence. That's how I would describe my attitude when I arrived at the hospital on Thursday morning, July 13th. We checked in at the Oncology floor. Soon after filling out the necessary paperwork we were taken to an examining room where I would meet the man that was in charge of saving my life. This was the doctor that came highly recommended by the doctor in Madison and now I know why. My doctor had a sense of confidence about him that many people do not have. He obviously knew what he was doing and that helped me to trust his decision-making.

The first decision he had to make was whether or not he needed to perform a bone marrow biopsy since the other one was done in Madison and he could not see the results for himself. I told him that I did not want to go through that again. After all, who wants a pen sized needle shoved into the back of their pelvic bone? Thankfully, he decided to skip this procedure and confirmed the diagnosis by looking at my blood under the microscope. That certainly helped me trust his decision-making. He knew that I had leukemia but he was not sure whether it was the most treatable kind, APL. Since this diagnosis came from Madison he needed to make sure it really was this type before starting treatment.

We began to discuss the treatment that I would be receiving. Of course, I knew that chemotherapy was part of the plan. The problem was that my **white blood cell (WBC)** count was too high to begin chemo. It was supposed to be less than 50,000 before they would start chemo otherwise I would be at risk for something known as **Disseminated Intravascular Coagulation** or **DIC** for short. So the first step was to start me on a drug called Hydroxyurea (Hydrea®) to lower the WBC count. This would begin later in the day.

My doctor would later tell me that when I checked in, I was on "the razor blade of life." He said that if he gave me too much or too little of any medication I would die. It was hard for me to imagine at the time that I was really that seriously ill because I felt alright.

After discussing the basics with my doctor, I was sent back to the waiting room until the hospital was ready to admit me. Around 11:00, my dad called and said that he had just arrived in Green Bay. He had cancelled his business appointment and driven straight through the night from Pennsylvania to be with me and my family. He made it to the hospital just minutes before I was taken to room 347, which would be my home for the next few days.

My new home was about as cozy as a hospital room could be. I had my own room and the nurse added an extension to the bed so that my feet did not hang off the end. Most people do not have to worry about that problem, but when you are 6' 9" you understand that most things in this world are made for shorter people. In a little while, I would get my first taste of hospital food and it was not very good. I felt pretty good at the time, and my family and I sat around and enjoyed one another's company.

Diagnosis Confirmed

Some time during the afternoon, the nurse practitioner came into my room to provide some more details about my treatment. She asked if I wanted my family to leave the room, but I told her I wanted them to stay. First, she told us that one of the side effects of chemotherapy is that it would greatly reduce our ability to have children. That was fine with us since death would do much more than reduce our chances, it would completely eliminate them.

Next, the nurse practitioner started stringing some long words together about the actual diagnosis. We had been hoping and praying that the Madison doctor was correct about it being the most treatable kind of leukemia. So I stopped her during her spiel and asked, "Wait a minute, is it the M3 type of leukemia?" When she confirmed the earlier diagnosis we all started crying – not because we were sad, but because we were so happy. I think this confused her because she thought she was the bearer of bad news, but we already knew I had leukemia. She must have thought we were crazy to be happy to hear that I had leukemia.

Lastly, she stressed the severity of my current condition. She said that my platelet count was at twelve. She said this was low enough for me to be at risk for internal bleeding – just sitting on my hospital bed! She said that if it dropped below ten, I would be at risk for brain hemorrhaging – just sitting there!

Later that afternoon, a nurse came into my room and explained that I needed to have a **PICC line** put in my arm. The PICC line would make it easier for the doctors and nurses to give me my intravenous (IV) medications and fluids. We were told it was a simple and easy procedure and nothing to worry about. They wheeled me down to a sterile room where I noticed several nurses and surgeons getting prepped. They handed me a form that I was supposed to sign before they could begin. It was called a "Permission to Resuscitate" form. In other words, if my heart stopped during the procedure, then I was granting them permission to take the necessary steps to get it going again. This would be the first of many forms I would sign which would permit a procedure that would put my life at risk. Nevertheless, it was a relatively safe procedure that is performed all of the time without complications, but it helped me realize the severity of my situation.

My parents stayed at the hospital with us throughout the entire day. At one point, my mother asked my doctor about what my treatments would be like down the road. In other words, what did he expect me to go through in the coming weeks and months? The answer both surprised and scared my mom. He told her that they were not making any long-term plans yet because they just had to see if I was going to live through the night. I knew that I was really sick but, at the time, I was not aware that things were that severe.

The next few days were not too bad for me. I still felt pretty good on the outside, even though I knew I was in deep trouble on the inside. I was hooked up to a few IV bags full of fluids and antibiotics. I had several friends and family members stop in to visit and I enjoyed getting caught up with them. One night, some of my former basketball team-mates stopped in, and we stayed up talking and laughing until almost midnight.

I believe it was crucial for me to maintain a positive atti-tude during my ordeal. One of the greatest helps in this area was to enjoy the friends and family members that visited. This kept my spirit boosted.

Even though I felt pretty good, I could tell that I was getting sicker all the time. My body began to swell up because I was not expelling the IV fluids as quickly as they were being put in me. I also threw up a couple of times on Friday night (July 14th). I had heard horror stories of chemotherapy causing people to vomit on a regular basis. Amazingly, these would be the only times in my entire bout with leukemia when I vomited. That says something about how far modern medicine has come in helping people deal with the side effects of chemotherapy.

It was also getting much harder for me to do any physical activity. I was getting very **anemic**. In other words, my red blood cell count was low. Consequently, my body was not receiving the amount of oxygen it required.

At this point, the main concern was to keep taking the Hydrea® medication to cut down the number of white blood cells. This seemed to work well on the first day. My numbers dropped from 68,000 to 53,000. They still needed to go below 50,000 before I could begin the chemotherapy treatment, but my numbers started climbing in the ensuing days.

Over the weekend, my doctor had been calling the hospital to check on my progress – or lack thereof. On Sunday night, he decided to pay a visit because he was very concerned about the ineffectiveness of the Hydrea®. My WBC count was back over 60,000, and we could wait no longer. He signed the orders to send me to the Intensive Care Unit and to start chemotherapy immediately. My easy days in the hospital had come to an end. It was time for the real battle to begin.

Hope in the Midst of Worry

One of the greatest struggles we have as humans is over-coming our tendency to worry about things from the unimportant to the very important. All of us struggle with worry at some point in our lives. Some people are consumed with it while others seem to handle it quite well.

It would be safe to say that I typically handle worry well, but now what would I do when my life was on the line. I was being wheeled to the Intensive Care Unit so that the nurses could do a better job of monitoring my health and be just seconds away in case something went wrong. This was no time to joke around with friends. My life was sliding down "the razor blade of life" and I was beginning to wobble off to the side.

Obviously, I was nervous about what was going to happen in the ICU, but I knew that it would not help matters to constantly fret and worry about it. I tried to focus on the things that brought joy in my life. I was blessed to have Casey constantly at my side. I often thought about what it would be like to face cancer alone as so many people have done. It would be extremely difficult.

As a Christian, I believe I had an extra source of comfort during this time. I believe that God was also there to comfort me. It's not as if I ever heard Him speaking to me to keep my spirits up, but I had a strong sense of conviction that He was not finished with me yet.

I knew that I was going to endure some painful times in the next few weeks but that He would see me through. I also realized that no matter how painful the situation, He could sympathize with me. After all, Jesus came to earth and was brutally beaten and crucified. He endured more pain than most of us could ever dream, and He did it for us. Think about that for a minute. The Creator of the universe (John 1:1-

3; Colossians 1:16) loves us enough to suffer unspeakable mental and physical pain, not because of something He had done, but to pay the punishment for our sins (2 Corinthians 5:21). I knew that I could not feel sorry for myself because, as a sinner, I deserved to suffer. Having this mindset helped me cast aside the worry that so often consumes people in tough situations.

My faith helped in another way, too. Since Christ has saved me, I know that when this life is over, I will be spending eternity with my Lord, and there will be no more sorrow, tears, suffering, or death (Revelation 21:4). I knew that if I took a turn for the worse and died, then I would be in heaven with Christ. I did not have a death wish, but I was not afraid to die. However, I was concerned about Casey and the kids.

As a Christian, I do not believe that we only have this life. I believe that all people will live eternally in one of two places: heaven or hell (Matthew 25:46). I know where I am going, so I had nothing to fear.

During His earthly ministry, Jesus offered some great teaching on the subject of worry. Luke 12: 22 – 31 records the following:

> Then Jesus said to his disciples: "Therefore I tell you, do not worry about your life, what you will eat; or about your body, what you will wear. Life is more than food, and the body more than clothes. Consider the ravens: They do not sow or reap, they have no

storeroom or barn; yet God feeds them. And how much more valuable you are than birds! Who of you by worrying can add a single hour to his life? Since you cannot do this very little thing, why do you worry about the rest?

"Consider how the lilies grow. They do not labor or spin. Yet I tell you, not even Solomon in all his splendor was dressed like one of these. If that is how God clothes the grass of the field, which is here today, and tomorrow is thrown into the fire, how much more will he clothe you, O you of little faith! And do not set your heart on what you will eat or drink; do not worry about it. For the pagan world runs after all such things, and your Father knows that you need them. But seek his kingdom, and these things will be given to you as well.

In this passage Jesus was teaching His followers to stop worrying about some of the things that we find ourselves worrying about on a regular basis: food, health, clothing, and so on. Jesus' advice was to stop worrying about those things and instead "seek the kingdom of God, and all these things shall be added to you" (v. 31). Now this is not an absolute promise that if you put God first then you will never be sick, hungry, or naked. That's not the point. The point is that God knows your needs and He will always be faithful to meet those needs when you are putting Him first.

In Matthew 25, Jesus told a story known as the Parable of the Talents. Jesus talked about three servants who were given varying amounts of money (a talent was an ancient form of money) while their master was away. Two servants worked hard and doubled the amount that their master had given, while one neglected his talent and buried it in the ground. When the master returned he had some exciting words for the first two servants who had worked hard for him. He said, "Well done, good and faithful servant...Come and share your master's happiness" (Matthew 25: 23).

Those words have been engrained in my mind for a long time. They are quoted in one of my favorite songs and I get excited about the day that I will hear from Jesus Himself, "Well done, good and faithful servant." Most people have a few slogans that they stand for or they live by. This is one of mine. I am motivated by the idea that I may actually get to hear Jesus say those words to me, and then I will enter into the joy of my Lord.

We worry about things when we allow ourselves to focus on the situation rather than the One who is in control of this world. I can vividly remember watching my mother spend countless hours watching the news during Operation Desert Storm because my brother was serving in the Middle East during that time (early 1990s). She was worried that something was going to happen to him. Of course, that seems to be a normal human reaction, and it would be hard to fault anyone for being concerned or worried about their child who has been sent to war. However, we must be careful to not let this worry consume us.

The best way to avoid being overtaken by worry is to take your focus off of the cause of that worry. Christians should be able to look to God during tough times and say, "Lord, this situation is beyond my control, so I am leaving it up to you." After all, we cannot be sure how things will turn out, but God knows. It might be that there was really no reason to worry in the first place. And even if there is a real reason for worrying, does it help the situation at all if we spend our time worrying about it? I suggest that during these times, a person needs to stop looking at the things of this world that so often give cause for worry, and start focusing on God instead.

There is a popular Christian hymn written by Helen H. Lemmel in 1922 that summarizes exactly what I have been trying to say. Read through the chorus of "Turn Your Eyes Upon Jesus" and think about how much easier it is to make it through worrisome times when our eyes are not focused on our own situation.

Turn your eyes upon Jesus,
Look full in His wonderful face,
And the things of Earth will grow strangely dim,
In the light of His Glory and Grace.

Truly the things of this world do grow strangely dim when we are focused on God and doing His will rather than being focused on our own situation. I was headed for the Intensive Care Unit and was about to find out whether or not I could do what I have just encouraged you to do.

Chapter 3:

The Intensive Care Unit

*"I love You, O LORD, my strength. The LORD is my rock,
my fortress and my deliverer; my God is my rock,
in whom I take refuge."*
- Psalm 18: 1-2

A Test of Faith

As a Bible teacher and pastor, I have often talked about the importance of trusting God through thick and through thin. When times are great, we should praise God and thank Him for His goodness. When times are tough, we should praise God, thank Him for His goodness, and lean completely on Him. Now, it was my turn. Would I practice what I so often have preached? Is it easier said than done? These questions would soon be answered as my faith was put to a serious test.

I was wheeled into the Intensive Care Unit (ICU) on Sunday night, July 16th so that I could begin chemotherapy immediately. When I arrived in my new room, I needed to get off the bed that I had been on for the past few days and get on the new bed in the ICU. It took a great deal of effort for me to stand up and then sit down on the new bed because I was so anemic. I was breathing very heavily after the transfer and decided to lay back and rest. The problem was that my new bed was shorter than the other one and I ended up smacking my head on the small headboard. Immediately, I closed my eyes and thought about how careless I had been. My platelets were so low that I thought I may have just caused some internal bleeding in my head. When I opened my eyes, the room was spinning – or so I thought. After a second or so, I looked at the foot of the bed and realized that the nurse was just wheeling the bed into its proper place in the room. This would be one of many humorous moments that helped me keep my sanity during the hospital stay.

I was hooked up to various devices so that the nurses outside my room could monitor my condition at all times. An **electrocardiogram** or **EKG** test was administered on Friday to check the condition of my heart. I believe this was done to make sure that I could handle the chemotherapy treatments that were about to start. I had an oxygen hose to help my body get enough oxygen since my anemic condition was severely limiting my ability to do that.

Later that night, a nurse walked in carrying a bag of bright orange fluid. This would be my first dose of chemotherapy. This particular chemo medicine was called **Idarubacin**. The amount of chemo that I would receive would be based on my size, and, since I am a rather large person (6' 9", 250 pounds), I was receiving a large dose (30 mg or 12 mg/m^2 of body surface area).

Allow me to briefly explain the goal of chemotherapy treatment for those readers unfamiliar with this medicine. When a person develops cancer, the cancerous cells begin to multiply and take over a portion of the organ, region, or the entire body. With leukemia, the cancerous cells infect the body's blood supply. Chemotherapy is basically a toxic substance that attacks both the cancerous cells and the healthy cells. The hope is that the chemo will wipe out all of the cancerous cells and leave enough healthy cells to start reproducing. It is administered directly through an IV site along with the normal fluids.

Having this basic understanding of chemotherapy made the entire process incredibly nerve-wracking. I remember watching the orange fluid slowly travel down the IV tube and thinking about the damage that this poison could do to my body. As it started to flow into my arm via my PICC port all I could do was hope and pray that it would do its job. To ease the tension a bit, my wife and I tried to imagine that it was Kool-aid or Tang being dripped into my line. There was nothing left for me to do except put it all in God's hands.

Most of the side effects of chemotherapy are not manifested until about a week later, but a few develop quickly. The first side effect that I noticed was an obnoxious case of the hiccups. It seems that everyone has their own method of getting rid of hiccups. I usually hold my breath for about thirty seconds and this often takes care of them. Not this time. I was able to get them to stop a few times, but each time someone asked me a question or a nurse touched my arm, they would start up again. It was one of those things where it was frustrating but laughable because it really was not a huge deal.

The next side effect of the chemo that I noticed was that it makes it hard to sleep. Of course, I was nervous about the poison being in my body, so that made it hard to sleep. However, chemo actually has the tendency to reduce the amount of sleep a person will get. This became a problem for me because I had been averaging about 2 – 3 hours of sleep per night for almost a week. This was likely due to a combination of being sick and nervous and trying to get used to different beds. Once again, I slept very little that night and was continuing on my downward spiral.

"I Won't Wake Up"

Monday marked my first full day in the ICU. The combination of Hydrea and chemotherapy was rapidly breaking down the white blood cells. I began to have a lot of trouble breathing during the day. They told me that much of the waste from this process was filling up in my lungs, so steps were taken to counter that problem.

I began to cough up some blood, and my breathing continued to worsen throughout the day. A respiratory therapist stopped in to check on me, and I was given a plastic device, called an incentive spirometry, to help me practice my breathing. It measured the amount of air that I was able to take in on a given breath. For someone my size, I should have been able to breathe in about 4.5 liters of air. In my critical condition, I was only able to get about .5 liters.

I knew that I was extremely sick and getting worse by the minute. I could not sleep due to my troubled breathing. During the afternoon, one of the nurses talked to me about the importance of getting some rest. I remember her saying the words "sleep deprivation." This began to weigh heavily on my mind so around 6:00 PM I decided to try to go to sleep for the night.

The next seven hours were going to be a huge test of my faith. I desperately tried to sleep, but all I could do was toss and turn. I knew that I needed to get some sleep, but I also knew that I was in real trouble. At one point in the evening I was taken in for an x-ray of my chest so the doctors could take a look at just how bad things were. While I was getting the x-ray, Casey called my mom so that she could be there, too, just in case things really went south.

By 10:30 at night, I was back in my room with Casey on my left side and my mother on the right. I cannot imagine what it must have been like to be in their shoes. Here I lay dying in front of their eyes, and all they could do was stay by me and pray.

Around 11:00 PM, I looked at my wife and said, "If I fall asleep, I won't wake up." I was not trying to scare her or make things worse for her than they already were. I just wanted her to know that I loved her and that this might be it.

My mind was racing. I believe wholeheartedly that a person can have full assurance of his or her salvation. Concerning the words of his first letter, the Apostle John stated, "These things I have written to you who believe in the name of the Son of God, that you may know that you have eternal life, and that you may continue to believe in the name of the Son of God" (1 John 5:13). As a Christian, I knew where I was going to spend eternity. I was not afraid to die, but I was concerned about my family. How would my wife raise two young children? What would it be like for my children to grow up without their dad? I trusted that God would take care of them. After all, He loves them more than I do and has limitless resources at His disposal to care for them. Certainly, they were in good hands. Those good hands were also taking care of me in my most desperate moment.

Little did I know that God had prompted some others to be praying for me at that specific moment. Nearly 2,000 miles away, in California, two of His faithful servants whom I had never met were praying for me. Who were these women, and why were they praying for me? I had been taking an online course during the summer from a school in California, and when I was diagnosed I was put on the prayer list. Within the next couple of days, I received an email from each of these ladies that not only demonstrated God's existence, but also His loving care for me. These two emails served as a source of encouragement to me because I knew there was no naturalistic explanation for this – God was involved in this situation. Take a look and decide for yourself.

Here is the first email:

I don't know if you receive the emails but I assume you do. I want you to know that you are continu- ally in my heart and prayers. Last night I couldn't sleep between 11:45-12:30 East Coast Time [I was in the Central Time Zone] and all I could pray for was you. I know…that God had called me to pray specifi- cally for you and your family during that time. I do not know if there was any urgency then, but God is faithful to wake me up and use me to pray when there is an urgent need. (from P.N.)

I was stunned when I read through this email. Not only was I humbled by the amount of prayers that were being said on my behalf, but this woman actually listed the time during which she was praying. This was during the same time that I told my wife that I was not going to wake up.

Here is the second email:

Thanks for your email. I know that God is granting all of you His special grace to get through this. When I checked the update on the website I saw that things were pretty rough specifically on Monday. Providentially all through the night I continued waking as I couldn't sleep very well just thinking about your situation, so most of the night I was up praying for you all. I couldn't help but wonder if Tim was in great need for prayer and that is why God kept me up all night. I see that he was having trouble breathing, sleeping, vomiting and just being troubled about leaving his family behind. (from M.S.)

This email was addressed to Casey. She had received an encouraging email a few days earlier from this woman. Casey responded to it and that is why M.S. thanked her for the email. She also mentioned the journal I had been keeping on the website. Throughout much of my hospital stay, I was able to type a daily report on my condition and what was going on with my treatment. On the days that I felt the worst, as was the case with this particular day, I usually waited a day or two before typing up the entry for that day. M.S. referenced my journal entry for Monday, but that entry was not posted to the website until late Tuesday night – after P.N. had sent her email! In other words, there was no possible way for her to know about the severity of my condition at that time, nor was there any way for M.S. to know about it. For some reason, these two women were praying for me during my darkest hour. I believe there is no other explanation for this than that God had laid it on their hearts to pray for me. I am so thankful they did.

In the past, I had heard numerous stories similar to this in which it seemed like God was the only logical explanation for what had happened. From a Christian perspective, some of these stories are believable because we trust that God can intervene in the world that He made. On the other hand, it seems like so many of the modern day miraculous claims are nothing but hoaxes perpetrated by someone seeking attention. Of course, whenever I heard one of these stories, I had no way of knowing whether it was true or false. Ultimately, it came down to whether or not the person telling the story was trustworthy and whether or not the story made sense. In my case, I knew beyond any shadow of a doubt that God was involved, and that gave me great hope. He was not finished with me yet.

Flat Lining

I remained in ICU until Friday. Thankfully, I do not remember much about it. I have had to check with Casey about many of the details of this chapter. I am not sure why I remember so little from the four days and five nights spent in ICU. Perhaps some of my medications were responsible. Nevertheless, I do remember some things.

One rather humorous moment occurred when an electrode came off my chest and my heart monitor flat lined. The nurses monitoring my vitals from the nurses' station could tell if something was wrong based on the activity or lack of activity on the heart monitor. They were aware that nothing serious had happened, so they took their time coming to my room. A few moments later, a nurse walked into my room to check on me. As she opened the door, I sat up quickly and exclaimed, "I'm flat lining." She looked at me and calmly stated, "Oh, you don't have to worry about that." Obviously, if I could say, "I'm flat lining," then I was not really too concerned about it. This was yet another humorous moment that helped me get through.

Hope in the Midst of Doubt

A proper mindset can go a long way in helping a person get through tough times. Proverbs 18:14 states, "a man's spirit sustains him in sickness." In other words, it seems that a person's mental well-being or mental attitude toward tough situations will help carry him through it.

Many studies have been performed concluding that a person's outlook has an impact on the outcome of their situation. Those with a good or positive attitude have a better chance of making a successful recovery. I am not advocating the so-called "positive confession" or positive thinking movement in which people can speak away or think away their illness. Not at all! Nevertheless, many researchers firmly believe that a person with a positive outlook will fare better than the one with a negative outlook. Some may chalk this up to their religious beliefs; others to serotonin levels. Whatever the reason, there seems to be a correlation between one's emotions and prognosis.

Of course, it is often very difficult to maintain a proper mindset, especially when everything seems to be going wrong. Perhaps the greatest enemy of this helpful outlook is doubt. When doubt seeps in it shatters one's confidence and leads to frustration, worry, and despair. How does one overcome this doubt?

Many Christians will tell you that during this time, they try to think about God's faithfulness and His promises to us. Oftentimes, as Christians, we like to think about passages like Romans 8: 28, which reveals that God works all things together for good to those who love Him. While I certainly agree with this, I hasten to add that the "good" may not always be what we expect. How many would consider the persecution endured by Christians and the executions that ended their lives as being good? The Apostle Paul wrote Romans 8: 28, and history tells us that he was beheaded for his faith. Was this for his good?

Before answering that question, I want to further clarify something that I mentioned earlier. Bear with me for a minute as I discuss something that may seem unrelated to this discussion but is actually very pertinent at this point. Many Christians have been influenced by a movement that promises its adherents that a believer should never be sick or poor. After all, they reason, since God wants us to be effective in doing His work, then He will always provide the health and resources necessary to be maximally efficient in doing that work.

This all sounds good from a human perspective. Who doesn't want to be healthy and prosperous? These teachers often claim that if one has the right attitude or speaks the right (positive) words in faith, then he will receive his or her healing and blessings from God. Some who teach this philosophy undoubtedly have good intentions and I have several friends who agree with this thinking; however, the Bible does not teach these ideas.

Hebrews 11 is widely regarded as the "faith chapter." Many have called it "The Faith Hall of Fame" because it highlights many of the Old Testament heroes and their incredible trust in God's promises. After commenting on spiritual giants such as Noah, Abraham, and Moses, the author of Hebrews summarizes the lives of others who had great faith. As you read about their lives, remember that they are included in "The Faith Hall of Fame" and think about whether or not they were blessed with health and prosperity. The author of Hebrews wrote that:

> Others were tortured and refused to be released, so that they might gain a better resurrection. Some faced jeers and flogging, while still others were chained and put in prison. They were stoned; they were sawed in two; they were put to death by the sword. They went about in sheepskins and goatskins, destitute, persecuted and mistreated – the world was not worthy of them. They wandered in deserts and mountains, and in caves and holes in the ground. (Hebrews 11: 35b – 38)

Please notice that some of these unnamed heroes of the faith were destitute, which means the exact opposite of prosperous. Some were stoned while others were sawn in two. Without trying to sound sarcastic, surely these are not to be seen as blessings of health and prosperity.

Some of you may be wondering why I just spent several paragraphs discussing this issue. I am not trying to grind a theological axe, but I felt it was necessary to clarify what the Bible actually teaches regarding a person's health, because I believe it has been misrepresented and distorted by this movement. Nowhere does the Bible promise believers that they will be free from pain, suffering, struggles, and poverty – this side of heaven. It is important to point this out because many have been led to believe that they should never experience financial hardships or poor health because they have faith. If people believe this, what happens to their faith when difficulties strike? Do they begin to doubt God's mercy and goodness? I hope not. It is more likely that they begin to doubt their own faith, and this is unfortunate. If they only had a proper perspective on these things in the first place, then they would understand that believers can experience both good and bad.

So let's revisit the question as to whether or not it was in Paul's best interest ("for the good" – Rom. 8: 28) to be executed. We could rephrase this and simply ask, "How can pain, suffering, and struggles work for the good of those who love God?" The answer to this question will be developed throughout the remainder of the book. To begin with, we need to look at Paul's perspective on the matter. After all, he is the one who stated that "in all things God works for the good of those who love Him."

The Apostle Paul wrote thirteen books of the New Testament[1] and could arguably be called the greatest Christian that has ever lived. His life was not one of health and prosperity, either. In 2 Corinthians he revealed some of the trials and tribulations he had faced as a faithful follower of Jesus Christ. I want you to see the sufferings that this great man of faith endured for the sake of spreading the good news. He wrote that he was

> I have worked much harder, been in prison more frequently, been flogged more severely, and been exposed to death again and again. Five times I received from the Jews the forty lashes minus one. Three times I was beaten with rods, once I was stoned, three times I was shipwrecked, I spent a night and a day in the open sea, I have been constantly on the move. I have been in danger from rivers, in danger from bandits, in danger from my own countrymen, in danger from Gentiles; in danger in the city, in danger in the country, in danger at sea; and in danger from false brothers. I have labored and toiled and have often gone without sleep; I have known hunger and thirst and have often gone without food; I have been cold and naked. (2 Corinthians 11: 23b – 27)

Once again, we can see that a faithful follower of Christ was not exempted from pain and suffering. In light of all this suffering, how was Paul able to maintain his faith in God? Did he begin to lose faith and start to doubt God? Not at all! I believe that if we can learn from his example, then we can learn to make it through the tough times that may lead us to doubt God's goodness.

It is crucial to see that Paul learned to see things from a heavenly or eternal perspective. He saw "the big picture" or at least tried to see it. He knew that this world was not his home and he longed for the day that he would be able to leave this world and be with his Savior. In his letter to the Philippians, he wrote:

> For to me, to live is Christ and to die is gain. If I am to go on living in the body, this will mean fruitful labor for me. Yet what shall I choose? I do not know! I am torn between the two: I desire to depart and be with Christ, which is better by far; but it is more necessary for you that I remain in the body. (Philippians 1: 21 – 24)

Paul believed it was "better by far" for him "to depart and be with Christ" than it was for him to "remain in the flesh." At the same time, he knew that God had called him to proclaim the good news. So as long as he was on Earth, he felt that he had a job to do, and, if that job called for suffering, then so be it.

Near the end of his life, Paul wrote a letter to his young protégé Timothy. Notice his outlook as he faced death:

> For I am already being poured out like a drink offering, and the time has come for my departure. I have fought the good fight, I have finished the race, I have kept the faith. Now there is in store for me the crown of righteousness, which the Lord, the righteous Judge, will award to me on that day... (2 Timothy 4:6-8)

Paul knew that he was about to be put to death, and he was not afraid because he knew he had done the things that God had called him to do. Having this same type of conviction helped me maintain a positive outlook during my bleakest hours. I have not done as much as Paul did, and I am quite sure I never will. Nor have I lived a perfect life, but I do believe that I have been pretty faithful to God.

The Apostle Paul and the heroes discussed in "The Faith Hall of Fame" (Hebrews 11) were able to exercise tremendous faith in God in the midst of incredible suffering. Is it possible for someone to do the same today? Is it possible for someone to avoid being consumed by their doubt? I believe it is, but we need to exercise a particular character trait that is sorely lacking in people today.

Confidence is really the antidote to worry and doubt. I was fortunate to have a doctor that was extremely confident. It seems that confidence is contagious because his confidence allowed me to feel certain that things would get better.

As a Christian, I have confidence that the Bible is true, and so, whatever it affirms is accurate. When it states that all things work together for the good, I believe it because I serve a God that cannot lie. I also believe that He will not allow me to go through any situation that I cannot handle with His help (Philippians 4:13). Now I promised that I would not spend a lot of time trying to convince you of my position until the final section, so I'll leave it at this for now. It is important for people to understand how far confidence can go in undercutting the doubt that is often so prevalent in tough situations.

Chapter 4:

The Roller Coaster Ride

*"Even though I walk through the valley of the shadow of
death, I will fear no evil, for You are with me..."*
- Psalm 23: 4

Still in the Woods

There's a phrase that people use when talking about still
being in a particular situation. They say, "We're not
out of the woods yet." That described my situation perfectly
on Friday, July 21st. The problem was that I thought I was
almost out of the woods, but the fact of the matter was that I
was still deep in them.

I was moved from the ICU back onto the regular floor,
and I was greatly encouraged. My numbers were getting
better, and I was almost done with the first round of chemotherapy – or so I thought. It's true that I was almost done

receiving the doses of chemo, but the side effects were about to hit me hard.

Saturday was supposed to be a lot different than it turned out. Casey and I had planned on attending a friend's wedding near Cleveland, OH. Following the ceremony, we were planning to go to Niagara Falls for a couple of nights without the kids. Instead of waking up in a place with beautiful scenery, I woke up in the same drab hospital room with a tree obstructing a large part of my view of the outside world.

Believe it or not, I was not too disappointed about this change. Of course, I would rather have gone to the wedding and then Niagara Falls, but God had different plans. I believed that He would allow me to use what I was going through to help others. Also, I had just been greatly encouraged by the two amazing emails from the women in California. I'm not sure that I would want to trade that experience.

Overall, the weekend was not too bad. The main problem was that I was having some pretty bad heartburn in the mornings, but it was usually gone by noon – thanks to the meds. My doctor told me that the heartburn was due to the chemotherapy. He said that it actually burns the soft tissue that lines a person's gastro-intestinal tract. He also said that if I could see the inside of my esophagus and stomach, they would look very raw.

I was able to have a few visitors during the weekend. On Sunday, I was able to shave and shower for the first time in over a week and I also had a haircut. I was feeling so much better than I had in a week and, on Monday, one doctor even told me that I would probably be able to go home in less than ten days. On Tuesday, I was unhooked from all of my IVs for a short time and allowed to walk down the hallway. I was still very weak and needed assistance from Casey to walk that far, but it felt great. I was at the top of the roller coaster and was completely unaware of the huge drop that was right in front of me.

The Plunge

(Readers with weak stomachs or who get queasy at the thought of blood should skip this section since it contains some gory details of what I endured.)

I went to bed on Tuesday night thinking that I had made it through the worst problems that I would see during this ordeal. I could not have been more wrong. I was hoping to get a good night's rest for the first time in a while. I had taken a couple of sleeping pills and expected to be out for the night. Regrettably, the worst of the side effects were about to start, and I was about to face the most miserable day of my life.

I woke up at one o'clock in the morning because I had started bleeding quite a bit in my left nostril. I have had countless nosebleeds in my life, so I was not too concerned at first. However, as time went on, I realized how dangerous the situation could get. My platelets and other clotting agents were still very low because of the chemotherapy. My normal methods to stop nosebleeds were not working so I paged the nurse.

The nurse had no way of knowing how bad this nosebleed was going to be. She gave me some expandable doggie bags and a nose clip. The nose clip did not stop the bleeding but only caused it to flow back into my throat rather than out the nose. I began coughing up large amounts of blood on a regular basis. Soon, my right nostril started bleeding, too. I tried to remain calm and do everything I could to get the bleeding to stop but nothing helped.

I continued to page the nurse on a regular basis to complain that something else had to be done since nothing was working. I remember yelling at her about it and trying to impress upon her the severity of my condition. I knew that my clotting agents were already low, but I was also very anemic. Now I was losing blood at a fairly steady rate. By seven o'clock, six hours after the nosebleed started, I had filled up five doggie bags with blood and tissues and there was no end in sight.

Finally, the nurse told me that she was taking me down to the emergency room to be treated. I was wheeled down to the ER but did not realize that things were about to get worse. The emergency room doctor treated me as a normal nosebleed patient and simply packed my nose with the same packing used on people who have a broken nose. Thinking he had solved the problem, the doctor sent me back to my room on the cancer floor.

The problem for me was that this did not stop the bleeding; it only diverted it once again to my throat. Another problem was that I could no longer breathe through my nose. This complicated matters for me quite a bit because the chemo had continued to eat away at the soft tissue in my GI tract. The rawness had moved up to my mouth, tongue, and lips. I no longer had the heartburn, but my mouth was like one giant ulcer. My tongue looked as if it had rotted, and my lips looked like giant scabs. To top it all off, I was now forced to breathe through my mouth, which kept it dry and irritated it even more.

I spent the rest of the morning and early afternoon fighting for air. The nurses felt as if the nosebleed had stopped or would stop soon because of the packing. What they could not see was what was happening behind the packing. As time went on, the blood began to slowly clot behind the packing in my left nostril. This did not stop the nosebleed, instead it started forming a large clot that grew like an icicle (only made of blood) dangling from the packing.

By noon, I had to keep my head in one position because as soon as I moved it, I started gagging and spitting up blood. I continually told the staff that they had to get the packing out of my nose because it was only making things worse. I told them that I was having a lot of trouble breathing. I'm sure they thought I was overreacting since, after all, it was just a nosebleed and things looked okay from the outside.

I continued to gag and fight for air. Finally, around three o'clock, a nurse came in and told me that she would take me to an ear-nose-throat specialist. I remember trying to move from my bed to the wheelchair. This forced me to reposition my head, and I gagged for several minutes and spit up a bunch of blood. This was the first time that the nurse had seen me do this, and I think she finally realized how bad things were.

I was wheeled to another section of the building to see the specialist.[1] Although it seemed like hours, I waited at the check-in desk for about fifteen minutes before being wheeled into an examination room. After another ten minutes or so, the specialist walked in to see if he could solve the problem and save my life. He asked me to open my mouth and immediately found the problem. The clot that had been forming like an icicle was clearly visible to him. He placed a tray under my chin and used a small vacuum to extract the clot. I could hardly believe what I witnessed. He pulled out the clot and set it in the tray. The clot itself was about the size of a hot dog. As soon as it was out, I spit up more blood. However, I could finally breathe a lot better.

Then the real fun began. He still needed to stop the bleeding so he pulled the packing out of my right nostril and sprayed a chemical into the nostril. It stopped bleeding almost immediately. Then he turned his attention to the main problem – the left nostril. He removed the packing, and, as he did, I gagged and spit up more blood. He sprayed the chemical in the left nostril but it kept bleeding. The next step was to cauterize it with silver nitrate. I had this procedure done a few years earlier, so I knew what to expect. However, the silver nitrate was ineffective because the wound was just too large.

The specialist told me that he was going to have to elec-trocute the blood vessels to get them to stop bleeding. Then he told me that I would not want any part of that procedure unless he first numbed the area. As he said that, he pulled out a needle that was several inches long. Casey told me she was shocked that they actually made needles that long for somebody's face. I really did not feel much from the needle because my nose was already numb from the chemi-cals. Soon after the needle, he had placed a small metal rod in my nose and his assistant was pushing a button on and off to fry the inside of my left nostril. It was not too long before he had finished his job. Nearly fifteen hours after it had begun, the nosebleed was stopped. The doctor proceeded to pack my left nostril with some biodegradable packing that he said would be gone in about a week. I could breathe again!

Rock Bottom

I felt that the long nosebleed was about as bad as it could get. The plunge had taken me to a point where there was no place to go but up. However, I had to stay at rock bottom before I could start going up again.

That night I was able to relax a little bit. I was exhausted from the nosebleed ordeal. Now my biggest problems were a high fever and the sores in my mouth. Other than those two things, I felt pretty good. I also had a chance to apologize to the nurse for yelling at her the previous night. I was glad that I had a chance to do that because I felt bad for losing my temper and taking it out on her.

Thursday was much like Wednesday night. Basically, I just had to deal with the fever and the mouth sores. Normally, the pain from these would probably be quite severe, but I was given a couple of pain patches to help me deal with that. Since I was receiving so many blood products, I had an appointment with an infectious disease specialist. They were concerned about the possibility of catching a bug or two since my immune system was virtually non-existent.

Shortly before eleven o'clock that night I had an allergic reaction to a blood transfusion they had given me. My whole body began to shake uncontrollably for about thirty-five minutes. I was shivering like someone who had just fell into some icy water (Yes, I know what this is like from an incident as a kid). This was a scary time because I really do not think I was cold, but I could not stop shaking. My teeth were chattering so much that I ended up biting down on my blanket to get them to stop. I did not know when it would end. The reaction finally ended around 11:30, and I was able to sleep pretty well that night.

Friday was inspection day because my fever indicated that I may have had an infection. First, I was taken to another room to undergo an **esophogogastroduedenoscopy** or **EGD** for short. This is a procedure in which a small camera is run down a person's throat so that doctors can get a look at the stomach and small intestine. Thankfully, the drug that I was given did not allow me to remember the procedure.

Later in the day, I was taken down for a **CT scan**. The whole idea of a CT scan was really interesting, and I was amazed at what we can do with modern technology. The scan results showed that part of the wall of my large intestine was swollen. This was possibly due to an infection.

An on-call emergency surgeon paid a visit to my room that night and explained what would need to happen if the large intestine ruptured. He told me that they would need to do emergency surgery to repair it. The problem was that my platelets were so low that any surgery would be life-threatening because I may not have stopped bleeding. I faced the very real possibility of being in a true Catch-22 situation.

On Saturday morning, I awoke to another nosebleed. This time it was my right nostril that was acting up – the left one was still packed. I stuffed some tissue up my nose and called the nurse. This time the nurses were not taking any chances. They immediately wheeled me down to the emergency room. The ER nurse pulled the tissue out of my nose and we were surprised to find out that the bleeding had actually stopped.

What happened next is not high on my list of favorite things that people have done to me. The doctor told me that she wanted to get a look at the clot. So she actually picked at it and when she did, my right nostril started bleeding again, but this time, it was more than before. She immediately grabbed some device and shoved it up my nostril to stop the bleeding, but this only made it worse. Next, she grabbed a small inflatable balloon that she shoved into my nose and inflated it. This was quite painful, but it seemed to do the trick.

Now, I was very frustrated. Both nostrils were packed and I had to breathe through my mouth again, which was even worse than before. I also had some strange looking device running out of my right nostril and taped to the right side of my face. I can still remember the confused look on Casey's face when she walked into my room that morning. Yet, no matter how strange it looked, the balloon had done its job.

I ordered a pancake for breakfast that morning and was only able to take a couple of bites because the sores in my mouth were so painful. For the previous few days I had only been able to eat chicken noodle soup. Now I could not eat at all. This would go on until Monday night when I was able to have some chicken broth and a few noodles.

I love eating food, so going three days without food was certainly no fun for me. The nutritionist often visited my room and tried to talk me into eating something. Of course, she was just looking out for my well-being. I told her that she could stop bugging me about it because as soon as I could eat, I certainly would do it. I actually got to the point at which I was so hungry that I would turn on the Food Network and watch other people eat. Strangely enough, this made me feel a little better. It would be close to a week before I could eat anything remotely solid. I ended up going from chicken broth to applesauce, pudding, and Jell-O to mashed potatoes.

Saturday night would be interesting. I was not sure how I was going to be able to fall asleep with both nostrils packed. I finally dozed off, but in the middle of the night my mouth closed and I panicked. I tried to breathe out through my nose and ended up ejecting the packing that was in my left nostril. At first, I was very concerned that it would start bleeding again, but it never did. I could actually breathe a little bit through my nose again. Other than not being able to eat, things were finally about to get better.

Hope in the Midst of Pain

Anyone who has undergone heavy doses of chemotherapy can testify to some of the painful side effects that result from the treatments. By no means have I tried to exaggerate or glorify the pain that I endured in an effort to gain your pity. That is not at all my intention for some of the details in the first half of this chapter. While I was in the hospital, I met others who suffered more than I did, including one whose diagnosis was terminal. Even though I endured some painful times, both physically and mentally, I realize that many people have had it much worse than I did.

So how does a person cope when dealing with pain? As an athlete, I have had my share of painful injuries – sprained ankles, broken wrist, etc. When these occur, we usually grit our teeth and try to tough it out. That might work with relatively minor injuries like these, but what about the awful side effects of chemo? Or worse, what about the mental pain and anguish that comes with a cancer diagnosis or the loss of a loved one? Can a person find or hold on to hope in the midst of these extremely painful situations?

I wish I could tell you that it was easy and give you a simple solution but, regrettably, there is no easy way out. I do not do a very good job of dealing with physical pain. I'm actually somewhat of a baby when it comes to that type of pain. Modern medicine has provided ways to deal with a lot of the physical pain; however, there is no real medical solution to mental pain other than masking it with drugs. Ultimately, a person has to deal with that pain.

I mentioned some of the mental anguish that I went through. I had to deal with hearing those dreadful words, "You have leukemia" and watch my wife's reaction to hearing those same words. I had to tell my mom and dad the bad news. I had a month-long hospital stay in which I had plenty of time to wonder whether or not the leukemia would take my life. The nosebleeds nearly took away my ability to breathe. It was certainly frightening to fight for each breath. There are many more stories that I could share that are not included in this book. Allow me to share some words of wisdom that helped me get through and may help you find hope in troubled times.

I have already touched on several keys to getting through. I was blessed to have so many people that cared for me. Casey was constantly by my side. Not only was her support encouraging but just having her there to talk to helped take my focus off the situation. My parents and some other family members were close by, and I received numerous cards and emails. The outpouring of love and support we received definitely helped keep my spirit up.

So much of our mental pain builds upon the worries and doubts about the future. When things are tough, it is hard to stay positive, and we begin to fear the worst. As those worries, fears, and doubts gain a foothold in our thoughts, it becomes harder and harder to see a way out. It is important to be able to deal with the worries, fears, and doubts when they arise or else they will continue to grow. The three previous chapters provided practical advice to overcome these things.

Another huge obstacle to overcoming the mental pain is to avoid the trap of self-pity. It is so easy to feel sorry for ourselves. We are experts at it. Because of our selfish nature, we tend to think that no one has it as bad as we do.

In reality, there is always someone who has it worse than you do (unless you happen to be that poor soul who is at the bottom of the list, which is highly unlikely).

Consider the story of Horatio G. Spafford.[2] He was an attorney who lost a fortune in real estate during the Chicago fire in 1871. About the same time, he lost his four-year old son to scarlet fever. Two years later, Spafford decided to travel to Europe with his wife and four daughters. He was delayed in New York with some urgent business, but he decided that his wife and daughters should get on the ship without him. He planned to catch up with them as soon as possible.

On November 22, 1873, the ship carrying Spafford's family, the *Ville du Havre,* collided with another ship and sank. All four of his daughters were lost in the icy waters of the Atlantic along with 222 others. When the survivors reached Wales, his wife sent him a message stating "Saved Alone."

Spafford immediately traveled to join his wife. As the ship passed near the spot where the *Ville du Havre* went down, the captain pulled him aside and notified him of their location. Spafford thought to himself, "It is well; the will of God be done." Shortly after this event, he penned the words to one of my favorite hymns – "It is Well With My Soul." Read through the words of this song and see if you can find

how Spafford could take comfort in God during his unimagi-
nable emotional pain.

> When peace, like a river, attendeth my way,
> When sorrows like sea billows roll—
> Whatever my lot, Thou hast taught me to say,
> It is well with my soul.

> **Chorus:**
> It is well with my soul, it is well,
> it is well with my soul.

> Though Satan should buffet, though trials should come,
> Let this blest assurance control,
> That Christ hath regarded my helpless estate
> And shed His own blood for my soul.

> My sin—oh, the bliss of this glorious thought!—
> My sin, not in part, but the whole,
> Is nailed to the cross and I bear it no more,
> Praise the Lord, praise the Lord, O my soul!

> And, Lord, haste the day when my faith shall be sight,
> the clouds be rolled back as a scroll:
> The trump shall resound and the Lord shall descend,
> "Even so"—it is well with my soul.

Did you catch it? Were you able to find Spafford's
source of hope? After all he had been through, how could he
proclaim, "It is well with my soul"? The first verse contains
a reference to the tragedy that took the lives of his daughters
– "when sorrows like sea billows roll." The next two verses

focus on his own salvation. He had confidence that Christ's death on the cross was sufficient to take away all of his sins. In chapter 2, I mentioned that I know where I will end up when I die. This is because I understand that Christ's death was sufficient to take away all of my sins, and that He has saved me from an eternity apart from Him. I believe there is something else mentioned in this song that provided comfort for Horatio Spafford.

Look at the fourth verse again. It is all about the return of Christ. There are two little words in the last line that are in quotations – "Even so". This is actually a quotation of Revelation 22:20, the second-to-last verse in the Bible. Jesus had just promised that He would return, and the apostle John responded by saying, "Even so, come, Lord Jesus!" (KJV). By citing this, Spafford indicated that he was looking forward to the time that he would be with Christ. He knew that at that moment his grief would end, and he would be reunited with his children.

For centuries, Christians have been comforted by the hope of spending eternity with Christ. They believed that a few decades of struggling on this earth cannot compare to the eternal bliss that awaits them after death. This hope has allowed Christians to endure some of the toughest situations that life can bring. This is not to say that Christians always handle tough situations properly, but they could if they would keep their eyes on Christ rather than on their current circumstances.

Chapter 5:

The Light at the End
of the Tunnel

"For everything that was written in the past was written to teach us, so that through endurance and the encouragement of the Scriptures we might have hope."
- Romans 15:4

Convalescence

The nosebleeds and mouth sores had made me miserable, but I was almost through the toughest part of my treatment. By Sunday, July 30th, I just needed to make it through a few more days without any complications. If I could do that, my doctor and I believed that I would be on the road to recovery.

I still had the inflatable device in my right nostril, but on Sunday afternoon, a nurse was able to deflate it a slight amount. This eased the pressure a little bit. It had been inflated so much that it actually made it more difficult for me to breathe through my left nostril. Breathing was finally getting easier.

I still had the mouth sores and was unable to eat anything. I had lost about 30 pounds since checking into the hospital. I have since jokingly told people not to try the "chemo diet." You can lose a lot of weight, but it just isn't worth the trouble. Things were definitely starting to improve. I had made it through the most difficult time in my life, and now I just needed to avoid any major setbacks.

By Monday, I was finally able to eat a tiny bit of food. I had a bowl of chicken broth and a couple of noodles. The balloon in my nose was deflated a little more, and breathing became much easier. Also, my blood count numbers were finally showing signs of improvement.

Monday was also the last day in July. Each of my rooms had a calendar on the wall. Every evening after midnight, a nurse would tear off the page from the previous day. I can remember seeing July 13th and 14th and 15th and thinking that the 31st might not ever come – at least for me. Now it read July 31, and I knew that it would soon be a new month.

This day also brought another lesson in perspective for me and for a couple of nurses. Green Bay was in the midst of a heat wave. I know that sounds strange to those of you that think of Green Bay as being "the frozen tundra," but it can have warm summers. The heat index on Monday was 110 degrees. A couple of nurses had complained about how hot it was outside and that I was lucky that I didn't have to be out there. I know they meant well, but I responded by telling them that I would gladly trade places with them. I had not been outside since the morning of July 13th, and I would gladly bear the heat and humidity for a breath of fresh air. They quickly realized that they were quite fortunate to be in good enough health that they could go outside. It just goes to show how easy it is for us to take the little things for granted. We need to learn to treasure every moment.

That night brought about another one of the many lighter moments we had during our time in the hospital. I mentioned earlier that we tried our best to stay relaxed and light-hearted. I received a couple of bags of platelets that evening because the chemo was still attacking the cells in my body, and my platelet counts were constantly dropping. The nurse and I had a contest to see who could come the closest to guessing my platelet count the next morning. I began the day at 30. She guessed the two bags would take me up to 55. I guessed 46. Now I don't mean to brag (actually, I do) but the next morning my results came back and my platelets were at 46. I would have preferred 55, but at least I got the satisfaction of winning that little contest. As I typed this information for the web update, Casey noticed it, and said that I was back to normal since I was bragging again.

By Tuesday, August 1st, I was really starting to feel better about my entire situation. The ear-nose-throat specialist came in to remove the balloon from my right nostril. I was very nervous that it would start bleeding, and I would be facing the same battle all over again. As he removed the device, it was obvious that it had done its job. I did not bleed at all and I could breathe through both nostrils for the first time in a week.

On top of this good news, I decided to try to get cleaned up. I took a shower – the first one in nine days. It is so easy to take certain daily occurrences for granted. Taking a shower was very difficult. First, I had to get unhooked from all of the IVs and wrap my PICC line port with plastic so that it would not get all wet. Next, the most difficult part was just standing or sitting up long enough in the shower to get clean. I was so weak that I could hardly stand for a minute at a time, so I was given a chair to sit on in the shower. Finally, I finished the shower and felt clean for the first time in over a week. I also had a haircut and shaved the little bit of facial hair that I still had – the chemo seemed to take care of most of it. This was probably the only positive side effect of the chemo, since I cannot stand shaving. Since I was in the mood to get cleaned up, I tried to brush my teeth. This turned out to be a very painful chore since my mouth was still one giant sore. I had not been able to brush my teeth for about two weeks because my gums may have started bleeding again and the sores made it too painful. All I could do was use a saline rinse several times a day. Things were finally looking up – or so I thought.

Minor Setbacks

Just as things were starting to look hopeful, I experienced a few obstacles to my recovery. My doctor happened to be on vacation during this week, and his replacement began to order some changes from the standard protocol to which I had been accustomed. Since I had learned to trust my primary doctor, I was not happy when these things were changed. We questioned the changes, and doubts started creeping in about my situation.

While this dropped my confidence, the appearance of petechiae all over my legs made it seem like I was starting the sickness all over again. Once again, my platelet count was to blame. The hospital staff was not entirely sure why my platelet count refused to rise. The doctor told me that my body may have begun to develop antigens which worked to fight off the platelet transfusions I was receiving. Rather than accepting the transfusions, my body was rejecting them.

He told me that if that was truly happening and my platelet count dipped much lower, they would have to find a blood donor that was an exact match for me – this was much more complex than a simple blood type test. They located a man who lived nearly three hours away and said that if my platelets continued to dive, then they would need to call him and ask him to donate immediately. I am thankful that I did not have to rely on this option.

Throughout the remainder of the week my platelet count looked like a sine wave on a graph. When I received transfusions of platelets the numbers would climb to 40-50 but would steadily drop down to the twenties over the next day. By Saturday, August 5th, my platelet problems were coming to an end. On Friday morning they were at 24 and had dropped to 21 by that evening. On Saturday morning, they had dropped all the way down to 18. Remember that a platelet count under 20 puts a person at high risk for internal bleeding while just sitting still. We were getting nervous about this drop, but at least they had only dropped three points every twelve hours. The doctor decided to forego another transfusion to see if they would recover on their own. Thankfully, by Saturday evening, the platelets had climbed back to 26. By Monday they were up to 47 on their own!

It is important to understand that doctors must consider each case on an individual basis when it comes to transfusions. I have been told that many oncologists will not consider a platelet transfusion until the patient's count is around 10. It is possible that I received transfusions at a higher number because of the amount of bleeding I endured.

On Thursday, August 3rd, Casey noticed that I had a rash breaking out on my shoulders and chest. This really did not bother me right away, but by Saturday the rash began to itch quite a bit. I was given a medication that would help reduce this irritation.

I was still struggling with the mouth sores, but things were getting better. Thursday also marked the day that I was finally able to try something that was a little bit solid. I had gone a full week without eating any solid food. Now, I was able to eat mashed potatoes, and on Friday I even ate a little bit of baked cod. Things were finally getting better!

Almost There

On Sunday, August 6th, I was in good enough condition to go for a brief walk down the hallway. When I say "good enough" I mean that I was able to stagger about 200 feet with Casey's help. It would have been funny to see a video of this since Casey is not quite 5' 4" and I am 6' 9" and weigh twice as much as she does. This short exercise was enough to take nearly all of my strength and energy.

This walk gave me a sense of freedom I had not felt for weeks. I had been limited to taking a few steps around my room a few times a day. All the while, I was hooked up to several IVs and had to be careful not to get my tubes caught on anything. I was about to experience even more freedom as the doctor gave the order to remove me from every IV. I still needed to take a few antibiotics orally, but at least I was finally free of the cumbersome IV stand.

My mouth had healed to the point that I could eat just about any food that I wanted to; however, I could not really taste anything. Nevertheless, I was thrilled that I could finally eat.

My doctor returned from his vacation on Monday and was very pleased with my progress. He told me that as long as I did not have any more setbacks, I could leave the hospital the next day. Of course, this was the news I was waiting to hear.

Tuesday, August 8th is a day that I will treasure and celebrate for the rest of my life. My doctor came into my room that morning and told me that I needed to pack my things because I was going to be released shortly. I just needed to wait for the necessary paperwork to be filled out.

I can still remember the emotions I felt as I tried to get ready to go home. I was so weak that I could not do much of the packing, so Casey did the lion's share. I remember putting my shoes on for the first time in four weeks and thinking how strange it felt to have something on my feet again, especially since my feet were a bit thinner than they were the last time I wore shoes. I remember climbing into the wheelchair for what I hoped would be the last time. I needed to wear a mask anytime I left my room, but even that could not hide the smile that graced my face as I was wheeled down the hall past the nurses' station. After saying goodbye to some of the nurses that had played such a large part in my battle, we boarded the elevator to travel to the first floor. As we headed toward the exit doors at the end of the hallway, I remember the exhilaration I felt to be making it out of the hospital alive. When I checked in, that outcome was questionable. Now I was heading toward the outdoors for the first time in nearly a month and my prognosis looked pretty good.

Casey pulled the car up and the nurse helped me get into the car through the passenger side door. After buckling in, we headed off to the pharmacy for some of my numerous prescriptions that I would be taking over the next few months. Although I was out of the hospital, I was still not cancer free. I would be going back a week later for another bone marrow biopsy to see if the first round of chemo had done its job.

Upon arriving at my parents' house, I took up refuge on the living room couch. I did not have the strength to go up and down the stairs on a regular basis, so I decided to stay in the room where most of the activity would take place. Several family members stopped in during the day to see me, and I enjoyed watching my kids play around. I had gone sixteen days without hugging my kids. The closest I had gotten to them was when my mother brought them to the hospital a few days earlier so they could stand on the lawn and wave to me. We were finally reunited and I savored every moment.

Hope in the Midst of Frustration

It is difficult to come so close to reaching a goal only to barely miss it. I felt like a greyhound must feel as it chases the fake rabbit around a track. During my last week in the hospital, I had come close to several goals only to be stymied by numerous setbacks. Throughout the majority of my hospitalization, I was considered **neutropenic** and could not receive visitors other than immediate family members. I was told that as soon as my **neutraphil** count remained above 1.0 for three consecutive days, I could have visitors. On a couple of occasions, my counts climbed above 1.0 for two consecutive days, but each time I dropped under 1.0 on the third day.

I have already detailed some of the other minor setbacks that occurred during this time. When combined with everything else that had taken place over the previous month, it was incredibly frustrating to go through these minor setbacks.

Webster's Dictionary defines frustration as "a deep chronic sense or state of insecurity and dissatisfaction arising from unresolved problems or unfulfilled needs." All of us have inevitably found ourselves in frustrating circumstances and have felt like the world was against us. If these frustrations are not handled properly, they can lead to anxiety and despair. How can one avoid these unwanted outcomes? What can we do to overcome these frustrations and find hope in the midst of them?

The Bible tells us that Jesus can sympathize with our weaknesses because He was tempted in all points as we are, yet He did not sin (Hebrews 4:15). Once again, we should strive to follow His example. If Jesus faced frustrations and was able to overcome them, then we should examine His example, so that we can discover how to avoid the consequences of allowing our frustrations to boil over.

First, I need to show you that Jesus did indeed face frustrating circumstances. He chose twelve disciples that repeatedly failed to grasp some of His basic teachings. For example, He often told them that He was going to be killed but would rise again (Matthew 20:19; 23:34; Mark 8:31; 9:31). No matter how often He explained this to the disciples, they continually overlooked this basic truth. Instead, they focused on their own ideas of what the Messiah would do. As a teacher, I can assure you that it is painfully frustrating to constantly explain a concept to students and watch them fail to grasp it.

This was not the only frustration that Jesus faced. On several occasions, He was confronted by some of the religious leaders that were more concerned with their own power and prestige than they were with the spiritual welfare of their fellow Jews. Although He had done nothing wrong, they kept trying to trap Him in some of His teachings. They even sought to arrest and kill Him. These things must have been incredibly frustrating for Him, especially when you consider that He had come to give His life for people that despised Him (Romans 5:6-8).

So how could Jesus avoid the temptation to allow His frustrations to boil over into despair? How was He able to face these situations without sinning? Of course, many Christians would provide the easy answer: that He was (and is) God. However, He also was (and is) one hundred percent man and as such faced many of the same struggles we do. As mentioned above, Jesus "was in all points tempted as we are" yet He did not sin. So there must be more to the answer than this.

Perhaps the first lesson that we can learn from these situations is that we should not place all of our hopes and dreams on people because they will inevitably let us down. When the inevitable occurs, we get frustrated with the person that let us down and with ourselves because we foolishly placed our hopes in someone that did not fulfill them. Sadly, many people get frustrated with God when it is really other people that have let them down. I have heard numerous people complain about Christianity because of the hypocrisy of its adherents. There is no doubt that many Christians are guilty of letting others down. In fact, we probably are all guilty of that. However, this does not mean that a person should allow that frustration to lead them to give up on God.

Second, we need to realize that certain frustrations will arise that are beyond our ability to control. There will be times when bad weather ruins a family's picnic plans or worse, it destroys a person's house or livelihood. It is important to recognize that we live in a world in which good things and bad things happen to "good people" and "bad people." As such, we should expect to have our best-laid plans occasionally thwarted. This is a part of life. When these times come, rather than dwelling on the frustrating circumstance, realize that everyone has had to deal with similar situations, and focus on maintaining a positive outlook. For example, I faced numerous frustrations while I was in the hospital. I know that I did not always deal with them in a proper manner, and now I can look back and laugh about some of them. My time in the hospital taught me an extremely valuable lesson in dealing with frustration. You see, I have also faced my share of frustrations since leaving the hospital, but now I have a little saying that puts the proper perspective on things for me. Whenever I catch myself complaining about frustrating circumstances, I say, "Oh well, at least I am alive to complain about it."

This may not seem like a profound point, but it makes a huge difference in how a person is able to deal with difficult times. Some people go through life thinking that life is all about their own happiness. If something makes them happy, then it is good. If something does not bring happiness, then it is not good. They often cling to a very self-centered view of themselves. Everything exists to bring them enjoyment. These are the same type of people that struggle to make it through frustrating circumstances in a proper manner. Other people realize that life is not all about them. There are some things that are bigger than their own happiness. For me, I realize that I have been given a second chance at life. I want to make sure that I spend my time making the world a better place for others. As a Christian, I believe this entails sharing the Gospel message with as many people as possible and encouraging fellow Christians to grow in their faith. At the same time, my little saying helps me remember how close I was to dying and reminds me to make the most out of every moment.

Finally, another key to dealing with frustration is to exercise patience. So often we allow minor inconveniences to frustrate us. Most of us have allowed our impatience to get the best of us when waiting for a few extra minutes during traffic congestion. If you are like me, then you can get a little impatient during these situations. It is in moments like these that you need to think about where this traffic problem stands in the grand scheme of things. Consider the fact that in most cases, the extra few minutes you spend are not going to make a big difference in your life. You could choose to use that time productively by praying. If you can remain patient and try to place the given situation in its proper perspective then you will have gone a long way in preventing frustration.

This approach does not just work with minor situations. It can help you deal with major circumstances. During my time in the hospital, it would not have helped my condition at all if I had allowed myself to get frustrated. I had to remain patient and put things in perspective. Sure I was going through a difficult time, and at times I did allow myself to get frustrated, but it did not do any good. I knew that if I did not make it through, then I would be with my Savior sooner. I also knew that if I did survive, then I would have been given a wonderful opportunity to reach out to others who are suffering in similar circumstances.

As I have shown throughout each of the chapters so far, having a proper outlook or mindset can go a long way in helping a person get through pain, frustrations, worries, doubts, and despair. I believe this is the primary reason that Jesus was able to endure His frustrating circumstances. He knew that He had not come to Earth to enjoy life to its fullest. He knew that He was here to proclaim the truth, and, ultimately, to die an agonizing death on a cross. He knew that He would face opposition. So when it came, He did not hang His head and give up. He faced it and kept His focus on fulfilling His goals. We should do the same in whatever circumstances we find ourselves.

What this really boils down to is that we need to be content. Contentment is an inner satisfaction that helps us find peace and acceptance in the midst of life's storms. Christians should find contentment in the fact that they belong to Christ and nothing can separate them from His love (Romans 8:38-39). Once that truth is realized, then nothing this world can throw at us should cause us to lose our contentment. Those who have not found contentment may find it very difficult to endure frustrating situations.

Chapter 6:

Out of the Hospital

*"Consider it pure joy, my brothers, whenever you face
trials of many kinds, because you know that the testing of
your faith develops perseverance. Perseverance must finish
its work so that you may be mature and complete,
not lacking anything."*
— James 1:2-4

Slow Progress

I had finally been released from the hospital. I was elated
to be able to spend time with family and friends, but I was
still not in the clear. My doctor had sent me home because I
was no longer in grave danger of becoming ill and he wanted
me to work on building up my strength. He scheduled me for
another bone marrow biopsy on the following Monday. This
would give me a little more than five days to relax and enjoy
my newfound freedoms.

I made a conscious effort to build up my strength. I had lost over forty pounds in a month and much of that was due to the atrophied muscles in my legs. Since I spent nearly all of my time in bed at the hospital, my leg muscles had gotten weaker and weaker. By the time I had gotten out of the hospital my legs were very thin. Casey helped me go for a walk every day to work on regaining some of that strength. On my first day out of the hospital, I was barely able to make it down to the stop sign at the end of my parents' block. Each day saw improvement, but I had a long way to go.

I was still taking several medications, including a chemo medication called **ATRA**. This was a medication that I took throughout my hospital stay and would continue to take until I was declared cancer-free. While this drug was sort of a miracle drug for my particular type of leukemia, it did cause quite a bit of joint pain, especially in my knees. Obviously, this hindered some of my progress.

Another area that I looked forward to working on was my diet. The mouth sores were finally gone, and I was no longer neutropenic. This meant that I could start to eat whatever foods I wanted to eat. It took several weeks before I was able to eat my normal size meals again. Also, many of the foods that I ate did not taste the same as they had prior to chemo-therapy. I was told that this is fairly common among chemo patients. Perhaps the strangest food for me to eat was bread.

Most food tasted normal again after about two weeks, yet bread had virtually no taste for me until about two months after I left the hospital.

Wearing the Mask

There is an old phrase that holds a great deal of truth. It says that "laughter is the best medicine." While it may not be the very best medicine in a given situation, I mentioned earlier that keeping a sense of humor certainly helped me get through my ordeal. There is another humorous story that I often share with people.

When I left the hospital, I was instructed by one of my nurses that I was supposed to wear a hospital mask whenever I left my parents' house. She told me that I would have to do this until she told me otherwise. I left the hospital on a Tuesday and faithfully followed her instructions. As Casey and I took our brief walks those first few days, I wore the mask. I remember walking to the park and watching my children play. I also remember seeing the way that some of the other kids looked at me. They must have thought I was pretty strange since I was wearing that mask.

On Friday, August 11th, the nurse graciously drove out to my parents' house on her own time to teach Casey how to change the dressing that protected my PICC line. While she was there, I asked her how much longer I would need to wear the mask. She said that she had called me on Tuesday afternoon and told me that I did not need to wear it anymore. Now I have absolutely no recollection of that phone call, so I told her that she didn't call. She said that she did, and that she had spoken to my mom first and then to me. My mom was there, so I asked her about it. I asked if the nurse had called on Tuesday and she said, "Yes." Then I asked her what she had said and my mom replied, "She said that you didn't need to wear the mask anymore." Then she told me that she handed me the phone and I talked to the nurse. Again, I have absolutely no recollection of that phone call. I must have been so tired from all of the events that day that I completely missed out on an entire conversation that I apparently had.

Of course, the funniest part in all of this is that my mom knew all along that I did not need to wear the mask, but she did not tell me. So I went to the park for a few days and probably scared a bunch of kids for no reason at all.

Back to Church

I had not been to church in over a month, and I was really looking forward to returning. It is interesting how things work out sometimes. I was scheduled to speak to some of the staff members at *Answers in Genesis* on July 21^{st,} but obviously that did not happen. Shortly after being diagnosed, I emailed the person that had arranged this for me to tell him that I had been diagnosed with leukemia and that I could not make it on the 21st. He told me that the staff would be praying for me. Little did I know that when he announced that particular prayer request to the staff there was a large group of people from a church in Green Bay who happened to be volunteering at the Creation Museum that week. One of the men from that group decided to contact me when he returned home. We have since become good friends and have spoken at a couple of conferences together. I decided I would go to his church for that first Sunday after getting out of the hospital.

This may not seem like a big deal to the reader and it might seem like a simple coincidence, but I believe that God had put it together to encourage me. When I looked at the bulletin for the morning service, I was excited to see the hymn "Holy, Holy, Holy" as the first song. This particular song is by far my favorite and I could not wait to sing it. After all, while I was in the hospital, I was not sure if I would ever sing any song again. As the music started, I tried to sing but could not. All I could do was sit down and cry tears of joy. I was simply overcome with emotion at being able to hear that song that so beautifully proclaims God's holiness.

This was another one of the many blessings God showered on me during that time.

Bone Marrow Biopsy #2

I have to admit, I really do not enjoy bone marrow biopsies. That probably does not shock anyone, especially if you know how the procedure works and what it feels like. It is about four minutes of strong discomfort and about 10 – 15 seconds of extremely intense pain. I mentioned earlier that I do not always handle physical pain very well. One day as I was complaining about having another biopsy, I told Casey that I really did not like them. She reminded me that she was glad to hear that, after all, if I did enjoy them, then there was probably something wrong with me. Good point!

On Monday, August 14th, I returned to the hospital to receive another bone marrow biopsy. The samples would be sent to the Mayo Clinic in Rochester, MN, for two particular tests: the hematological and the molecular. I was told that the hematological test was basically an examination of my blood under a microscope while the molecular test was quite advanced. It could detect one bad gene in 10,000 (recently I saw a report that moved this number to 100,000). A negative test result on both tests would mean that I was in full remission.

We did receive some encouraging news on that day. My platelet count had risen to 457 and all my other numbers were fairly normal. My doctor jokingly told me that I should become a platelet donor. Also, based on my counts, he expected the test results to come back negative, so we were quite hopeful.

The test results would take about a week to arrive. That being the case, my doctor instructed me to work on getting my strength back but not to overdo it. So I spent the rest of the week hanging around at my parents' house and enjoying time with my family. I tried to do things that would make life seem normal again. It was really strange to think about doing things for the first time since leaving the hospital. Each time I was able to engage in a normal activity, I counted it as a blessing that I was able to enjoy that activity again. We went to church, did a little bit of shopping, and even took my son to a movie. I was still very weak, but each day brought marked improvement.

Surprise!

On Thursday I had a checkup and found out that my numbers were still pretty good. I was given permission to go home for a day. Casey and I had not seen our home since July 12th, so we were anxious to get back, even if it was only for one day. We never had a chance to pack our own things since we had some friends stop by the house and bring everything to Madison where we had been waiting.

On Thursday night we had some of our closest friends over for dinner and then spent the rest of the evening talking about what I had been through. We laughed about so many of the situations I was in and just had a wonderful time getting caught up with them. One of the families had actually driven all the way to Green Bay a couple of weeks earlier to visit me in the hospital. The problem was that by the time they arrived, I had just been given a shot of Benadryl and was almost completely "out of it." That also made for a humorous moment because I could hear the entire conversation but was so tired from the drug that I could not even open my eyes for more than a few seconds. So Casey had to do most of the talking while I faded in and out of consciousness.

On Friday morning I was able to visit my school to surprise my co-workers who were having their second day of in-service. Only two of them knew that I was coming, and I planned to show up in the conference room shortly after their meeting started. They had been praying for me continually, and I wanted them to see that I was up and around and, hopefully, on the road to recovery. Casey and I showed up at the right time. I walked in and asked if they had room for two more people. I have to admit, they were very surprised to see me. For the next twenty minutes or so, I was able to explain to them what was going on and thank them for their constant prayers. I was so thankful for the opportunity to see them all again. After saying good-bye to everyone, it was time to head back to Green Bay because my doctor was keeping me on a short leash. For obvious reasons, I was not allowed to be too far from the hospital for any considerable length of time.

One Out of Two Isn't So Bad

We arrived at the hospital for my appointment on Monday, August 21ˢᵗ, with high hopes but braced ourselves for the worst. My doctor told me that the hematological test had come back negative. As mentioned earlier, this basically means that they could not see any cancer cells under the microscope. That was awesome news, especially when you consider that the cancerous cells were easily detectable under the microscope just one month earlier.

That was the good news. The bad news was that the molecular test had returned positive. This meant that I still had leukemia, but there was a silver lining. My doctor told me that the amount of bad cells was just a tiny fraction of what it was when I checked in. In other words, the chemo treatments were doing their job, but I was not finished with them.

Chemotherapy – Round #2

Soon after hearing the news about the test results, I walked to the nurses' station so that I could get started on the second round of chemotherapy. The plan was for me to receive the same type of chemo drug (Idarubacin) but only forty percent of what I received the first time around.

My doctor was confident that this round would be much easier to get through. First, I was receiving less chemo than the first time. Second, I was in much better shape than the first time, even though I did not feel like it. When I checked in on July 13th, I felt strong and healthy. Now, I felt weak and sick. However, on the inside I was in much better shape. He told me that when I checked in I was "as sick as a dog."

We waited in the nurses' station for a little while as the chemo was being prepared. We had a little mix-up with the amount of Idarubacin that I was supposed to receive. During my month in the hospital I was repeatedly told that I was receiving 12 milligrams and that I would only be receiving 5 milligrams during the second round. When we saw the syringe of Idarubacin it was marked at 12 mg. It didn't look like the same amount I was receiving during the first round, but it was marked the same. I questioned why it was 12 mg when I was told all month (and even by my doctor in the morning) that I was going to receive 5 mg. The problem was that they were not using the full label. In the hospital, I was actually receiving 30 mg of Idarubacin, which is equal to 12 mg/square meter of body area. The 12 mg that I received during the second round was equal to 5 mg/square meter of body area. So, if any of my former chemistry students are reading this, now you know why it is so important to always have the proper unit along with your number.

Once we got to the bottom of that confusion, it was time for the chemo to start again. My biggest fear was that the chemo would not be effective enough to wipe out all of the bad cells. My second greatest fear was that I would have to go through the mouth sores and nosebleeds again. As the nurse sat down to administer the chemo, I suddenly had a new fear. During my first round, all of the chemo was administered via an IV drip. For this round, and the two subsequent rounds, it was administered by the nurse pushing it in through a syringe. Now, I know that the nurses are well-trained and very good at their jobs, but I couldn't help but wonder what would happen if one of the nurses suddenly had a muscle spasm and forced a bunch of chemo in all at once. Since the PICC line through which the chemo entered my body went through the main blood vessel to within a couple inches of my heart, it would mean that all of that chemo would go straight into my heart. That was a bit unnerving, but, like I stated, they are well-trained, and I don't think the above situation has ever really happened.

Perhaps the best part of the second round was that it could be done on an outpatient basis, as long as I stayed healthy enough. Each day from Monday through Thursday saw me in the nurses' station for a couple of hours while I received the second round of Idarubacin. For the most part I felt pretty good. I was still weak but was gaining strength each and every day. I had a good friend visit me during the week, and we ended up taking the kids to a small amusement park in Green Bay and then going to a birthday party on Thursday night. I had probably overdone things a bit. During the party, I remember just lying on the couch because I was very uncomfortable. People have asked me what it was like to have chemo, and for a while I didn't know how to describe the feeling to them. Finally, I decided that it was like being poisoned. Not that I would know, but since chemo is poisonous, it probably is an accurate description. I just ached. Other than some pretty bad heartburn, the pain was not localized. I just hurt all over.

As a result of that feeling, I decided that I was just going to take it easy over the next week. Since many of the side effects of the chemo do not manifest themselves until about a week later, I knew that the next few days would be crucial. I hoped and prayed that I would get through it without the mouth sores and nosebleeds.

Thankfully, I was able to make it through the second round of chemo without any major complications. One of the nurses suggested that I should chew on some ice while receiving chemo treatments. I am not sure if this had any effect, but in theory, it should cause the blood vessels in the mouth to constrict, thus reducing the amount of chemo going through the blood vessels in the mouth. I experienced a few minor side effects, but for the most part I was able to focus on everyday life rather than just trying to survive. As expected, my blood count numbers dropped significantly, and I spent a few days being neutropenic.

We were able to go home for a few days with the kids. This was a huge blessing because the kids had become extremely homesick. Kayla was able to start her school year – two weeks late – and Judah was able to play with some of his toys for the first time in nearly two months. Both of them were thrilled with these new developments, and Casey and I were just happy to have a small taste of normalcy again.

The second round of chemo had come and gone. It was a difficult time but was a vast improvement over the first round. Now, we had to wait to find out whether or not the chemo had done its job. I was scheduled to go in for my third bone marrow biopsy on Monday, September 11th and we were cautiously optimistic.

Hope in the Midst of Trials

Getting out of the hospital was a huge thrill, but finding out that the leukemia was still present was very disappointing. Not only did it mean that there would be more difficult times ahead, it also meant that the cloud of cancer, along with its potential to kill, was still over my head. I knew that I had many more trials to come.

There are several ways to define the word "trial." One of the definitions found in Merriam-Webster's is "a test of faith, patience, or stamina through subjection to suffering or temptation." To call a cancer diagnosis and its subsequent treatments a trial is probably an understatement. Nevertheless, all of us face trials at one time or another. How can we make it through these situations? How come some people handle these situations well, and others do not? If there really is a loving and all-powerful God, then why does He allow those who love Him to go through such awful situations? Once again, these are great questions. I will deal with the first two in this chapter and the final question will be dealt with in the final three chapters of this book.

There are a number of possible reasons why some people deal with trials better than others. It would not be fair to say that Christians always do a better job than non-Christians, because there are some Christians and non-Christians who do a great job of dealing with trials. At the same time, there are also some in each group that do not do a great job during these times. So the answer must be a bit more complex than that.

I think it would be accurate to say that those who deal well with trials do so for different reasons, but they all have one thing in common: perseverance. Perseverance is the ability or drive that a person has to "stay in the fight" even when you may have seemingly legitimate reasons for giving up. It is what some athletes have dubbed "stick-to-it-iveness." A person whose character includes this trait is able to focus on the goal rather than on the difficult circumstance itself.

Life is full of examples of people who have exercised this ability. Think of a young student who excels despite difficult surroundings, learning disabilities, and/or inadequate training. Perhaps it is an athlete who continues to strive to play despite being setback by serious injuries. Perhaps it is the person who pulls himself up by his own proverbial bootstraps. Or maybe it is the soldier that refuses to give up after being wounded and continues to put himself in harm's way to save his fellow soldiers and people. In addition to many other qualities, these people have all demonstrated perseverance.

This is what is really needed during a cancer diagnosis. For some people, the natural response would be to give up, get down, and engage in self-pity. Of course, unless you have been in their shoes, it is unfair to criticize them for that. However, there is a better way. Those who exhibit perseverance would look at their situation and say "bring it on." They recognize that life can be difficult, but they refuse to let that stop them.

I believe the vast majority of people who have been diagnosed with leukemia or any other form of cancer do display perseverance. They suddenly find themselves in one of the most devastating situations you could imagine and they shine. Recently, I was talking to a woman whose daughter is studying to work with radiology patients. Before interning in that area, the young woman dreaded the idea of working with people who were so sick. Within three days of being in that area, she said she had found her calling. She knew that she wanted to work with cancer patients for the rest of her life because they had such a tremendous attitude. She said they were fun, determined, and optimistic. I found the same thing to be true for most of the people that I have known who have battled or are currently battling this disease.

Perhaps the most amazing story of perseverance that I have ever seen is about Dick and Rick Hoyt.[1] For those unfamiliar with their story, here is a brief synopsis. Rick Hoyt was born with severe handicaps. He cannot walk or speak but communicates through the use of a computer in which he "types" the letters by using his head to select letters. In 1977, Rick "told" his father Dick that he wanted to compete in a five-mile benefit run for a local lacrosse player that had been paralyzed in an accident. Dick was not a long-distance runner, but he began training.

Within four years, Team Hoyt entered the Boston Marathon and finished in the top quarter of the field, with Dick pushing Rick in a special wheelchair the entire way. As if that was not enough, they began to compete in triathlons. During the swim, Dick swims with a rope around his waist that is attached to the boat that Rick is in. For the bike, Rick sits in a special seat in front of the handlebars. As if that still was not enough, Team Hoyt has completed six Ironman triathlons. Are you ready for this? An Ironman consists of a 2.4 mile swim, a 112 mile bike ride, followed by a full marathon run of 26.2 miles…all in one day! This incredible test of endurance is an amazing accomplishment for just one person. Imagine pulling, carrying, and pushing another adult around the entire race!

Obviously, to participate in these events, both of the Hoyts have had to display tremendous perseverance. Dick has had to train relentlessly to be able to compete as he does.

However, according to their website, Rick is also quite the competitor. Rick had to persevere through a childhood full of closed doors. Since he could not communicate, many people thought he was a "vegetable"[2] (which is a horrible term to describe someone made in God's image). He wanted to go to school and be like everyone else. Rick not only ended up convincing the school to let him enroll, he eventually graduated from high school and went on to college where he earned a degree in special education from Boston University. He has been working with a team to develop a computer that people in his condition can control with their eyes.

The Hoyts have continually displayed that "never say die" attitude that is the true mark of perseverance. Rather than allowing the school's rejection of Rick get them down, the Hoyts found a way to make it work. They pushed on long after others may have quit. This is the attitude that people need to possess if they want to successfully deal with difficult circumstances, such as a cancer diagnosis.

The Bible instructs Christians to persevere. The Apostle Peter instructed his readers that God has given believers everything they need for life and godliness. As a result, Peter says that we need to "make every effort to add to your faith goodness; and to goodness, knowledge; and to knowledge, self-control; and to self-control, perseverance; and to perseverance, godliness; and to godliness, brotherly kindness; and to brotherly kindness, love" (2 Peter 1:5-7). He goes on to say that if you possess these qualities, then they will keep you effective and productive in the knowledge of Christ. Perseverance is one of those traits that a Christian should exhibit because life is tough and God wants His people to be examples that other people can follow.

Also, in the passage cited at the beginning of this chapter, James instructed believers to be joyful when they face trials because the testing of one's faith produces perseverance. I have faced a fair share of difficult circumstances in my life. Sometimes I have handled them well, and sometimes I wish I could go back and respond differently. Nevertheless, I can look back on those times and see how they prepared me for what I was currently facing. I knew that I had to persevere. I had a family that was counting on me to make it through, and I also believe that God would want nothing less than for me to persevere in the midst of trials. As I stated earlier, I had a strong feeling that He was not finished with me yet.

Chapter 7:

The Recovery

Praise the Lord, O my soul; all my inmost being,
praise his holy name. Praise the Lord, O my soul, and
forget not all his benefits - who forgives all your sins
and heals all your diseases..."
- Psalm 103:1-3

Bone Marrow Biopsy #3

I arrived at the hospital for my third bone marrow biopsy on Monday, September 11th. Prior to this appointment, I had asked the nurse practitioner if there was anything I could take to reduce some of the pain during the biopsies. She prescribed an anti-anxiety medication known as Ativan® for me because she said it would make me "happy to be there." I had taken the prescribed dose an hour before my appointment, just as instructed. The nurse practitioner asked me if I was "happy to be there," and I told her that I did not notice any change. She sent me to the nurses' station to receive another dose of the drug intravenously.

Once I was adequately drugged, I returned for my biopsy. This time around it was a little easier to endure. While the drug had not taken away a lot of the pain, it did take a little bit of the edge off and helped me relax. This was important in the healing process, too. Following my second biopsy, my back was very stiff for a couple of days; however, because I was more relaxed, my back never really stiffened up after the third biopsy.

We also learned another valuable lesson that day. When a drug label mentions that you should not operate motor vehicles while taking the drug, it is important to follow that advice, no matter how well you think you might feel. Casey drove us home from the hospital, even though I told her that I felt good enough to drive. We stopped at a drug store, a restaurant, and then headed home. Once we got home, I took a long nap. When I woke up, I asked Casey how we had gotten home because I had very little recollection of the drive. If I had driven, we may have ended up in an accident.

Once again, the samples from the bone marrow biopsy were sent to the Mayo Clinic. We were told that the results would be back in a week. My blood count numbers were good enough for us to return home for the rest of the week. We were really looking forward to spending a larger amount of time at home, and now we had nearly a week. We were scheduled to return on Monday the 18th to find out the results of the biopsy and to start the third round of chemotherapy. The 18th happens to be my daughter's birthday. She told me that the best gift I could ever give her was to tell her that I did not have cancer anymore.

Remission!!!

We spent the next few days around the house trying to get caught up on miscellaneous things that were neglected during my hospitalization. On Friday, September 15th, Casey and I were preparing to head to my school to watch a volley-ball game. I had been longing to see my fellow teachers and my students again, but had only been given one chance to do that until then. As much as I wanted to do it a couple of times earlier, Casey would not let me violate my doctor's orders to stay away from crowds when I was neutropenic. We had planned to go to a couple of other games to see everyone, but each time my numbers came in just below the minimum level.

I was getting dressed when I heard the phone ring. I heard Casey talking into the phone as she walked up the stairs and into the room. She hung up the phone and then told me some words that I will never forget. I'm still not sure how she maintained a straight face as she said, "That was the doctor. You're cancer free!" I vividly remember throwing my hands up into the air and falling back onto my bed. I was so excited, but all I could do was cry tears of joy and thank God for taking care of me and seeing me through the entire ordeal.

Like the previous biopsy results, the hematological test came back negative. However, unlike the previous results, the molecular test also came back negative. This meant that, using today's most advanced methods to detect leukemia in the cells, the machine could not find one bad gene out of 100,000. As far as my doctor was concerned, I was in remission. Those words were fun to type so I will do it again: I was in remission!!

We finally left to attend the volleyball game. I could not wait to tell everyone the wonderful news. As we drove to the game, I called my parents to tell them the news. Just two months earlier, I had to tell my mom some of the worst news that she could imagine. Now, I was able to tell her some of the best news. We arrived at the game and had a magnificent time talking to people. People kept asking me how I was doing, and I could actually tell them that I was doing awesome. I was in remission!!

More Chemo

Although my prognosis had instantly become much better, I knew that I still had several more difficult weeks ahead of me. I was still scheduled to begin my third round of chemotherapy on Monday, and it was going to be a tough round.

Many people have asked why I still needed to go through two more rounds of chemo once I was given the "all clear". I have to admit that I also asked that question several times. I decided that there were a couple of reasons to proceed this way. First, my doctor had done a great job at restoring my health already, so I was willing to trust him with the next step. Second, the protocol for my type of leukemia was to go through the entire four rounds. Research had demonstrated that this was the best way to treat what I had. Finally, I wanted to make sure that all of the leukemia was gone. While the molecular test provides extremely precise results, there was always a chance to have a little bit of the bad cells remaining in my system. A third and fourth round would hopefully kill off any of those cells that might still be lingering.

For the third round of chemo, I was given a different type of chemo known as **Mitoxantrone**. Instead of being bright orange, like the Idarubacin I had been receiving, Mitoxantrone is very blue. It almost looks like ink. We were told that one of the potential side effects of the drug is that it could have turned the whites of my eyes blue for a while. As long as there was not any pain or long-term negative effects of this, I was actually hoping it would happen so that I could take a picture to show people. Well, it never happened.

I received doses of Mitoxantrone on five consecutive days. The total dosage was equal to what I received during my first round of Idarubacin. I knew that this round would be tough, and once again I hoped and prayed that I would be able to avoid any major complications. Thankfully, I did avoid serious side effects.

As expected, my numbers did dive, and I was admitted into the hospital from Friday, September 29th, until Tuesday, October 3rd. This was merely a precautionary measure since my numbers had bottomed out. My doctor did not want to have me risk getting any infections since I had little to no immune system. I was not hooked up to any IVs, and this brief hospitalization was almost completely different than the first one. I felt good and basically treated my stay as though I was stuck inside a hotel room for a few days.

During this time, I received some shots of Aranesp to stimulate the development of red blood cells. My energy level was extremely low, so my doctor wanted to be sure that nothing was wrong with my heart. I also had to undergo a **MUGA scan**. This test measures the amount of blood that the left ventricle of the heart is able to push out. The result was a 52, which is on the very low end of being normal. We concluded that my low energy was primarily a result of being anemic from the low red blood cell count.

We stayed in Green Bay for the remainder of the week while I tried to gain strength. On Monday, October 9th, I had another appointment to check my numbers. My red blood cell count was still very low, and dropping, but everything else was getting better.

Also, I was made "the happiest man alive" (nurse's words) by having my PICC line removed from my arm. The PICC line was certainly helpful while I was undergoing the more intensive parts of my treatment. After all, it was much easier for a nurse to hook up a syringe or IV bag to the port than it was for them to stick me with a needle every time. However, now that I did not need as many treatments, I asked whether or not it could be removed. I was fortunate to have my PICC line in my left arm. Some people need to ports placed on their chest or in their forehead. Mine was probably the easiest to deal with, but it was still annoying. The dressing needed to be changed weekly. I had to wrap my arm in plastic and seal it with tape any time that I wanted to shower. Also, I constantly had two plastic pieces rubbing against the side of my chest when I tried to sleep. To have the port removed really helped me feel as though I was completely healed. It also left five tiny scars (four from the stitches holding the port in place and one from the actual line) that are always there to remind me of my entire ordeal.

After having the port removed, we moved home. Other than a couple more appointments, most of my checkups could be done at the local clinic. I spent a good deal of time at the clinic over the next few days because I had to receive some blood transfusions. I was very pale due to the low red blood cell count, but the two transfusions really helped pick me up.

On Thursday, October 19th, I was back in Green Bay for another MUGA scan. Once again, my doctor wanted to make sure that my heart was in good enough condition to continue with the treatments. He was concerned since the first test showed that I was just barely in the normal range. The second test showed that things had improved a little bit. My MUGA scan results showed that my LVEF (left ventricle ejection fraction) was up to 56.6. This was nearly five points higher than the first test. However, my doctor was still not convinced that it was good enough to proceed to the final round of chemo. He called a cardiologist to talk things over with an expert. The cardiologist told him that since I had two "normal" results from the MUGA scans and was in remission, then he should proceed to give me my last dose of chemo.

The news was a little bittersweet. Obviously, I was thrilled that my heart was operating in the normal range. At the same time, part of me seemed to be hoping for a little lower result so that I would not have to go through chemo again. In the end, I was really hoping for good results on the MUGA scan and being done with chemo. Even though chemo is very tough on the body, I did not feel missing one final dose was worth having a weakened heart.

Once again, the chemo was administered at the nurses' station. Three months earlier I had been in the Intensive Care Unit receiving my first dose of chemo. My life was hanging in the balance and we were all quite nervous. Now, I was sitting in the nurses' station, talking to those around me, and enjoying a sub sandwich while the chemo was going in through an IV. That was quite a contrast.

The fourth round of chemo was by far the easiest to cope with. My numbers dropped a bit, but I was never neutropenic. In fact, I was able to attend a conference in St. Paul with a good friend and his youth group. During this trip, I also had my first opportunity to share my testimony contained in this book, including the nosebleed and blood clot story. The youth loved that one – at least the boys did. It felt great to have the opportunity to minister to young people again.

Back to Work

The fourth round of chemo had come and gone. The next big step that I needed to take was to return to work. On the day I was diagnosed, I was told that I would not teach again during that year. Yet, less than four months later, I was back in the classroom on a part-time basis.

I returned to work on November 6th, and I could not have been more thrilled. I taught two classes in the morning and then spent the rest of my day in the school's conference room studying, reading, and resting. A lot of people were very concerned about whether or not I was overdoing it, but I felt great. In fact, I probably did overdo it on my first two days by staying late in town both nights for various reasons. However, I was too excited to get worn out. I had come from "the razor blade of life" and was now given another chance to do what I love doing.

I continued to teach part-time for the remainder of the first semester. When the second semester started, I resumed working full-time and finished the school year without any complications. I still had quarterly checkups complete with bone marrow biopsies. Finally, in December 2007, I was told that I no longer needed to undergo biopsies. The same results could be obtained through a blood draw. As of May 2008, I only need to go in for six-month checkups.

Triathlon Training

My body had been through a horrible four-month battle with leukemia and its subsequent treatments and side effects. I am not the most physically fit person in the world, but I do like to maintain a degree of physical fitness. At first, I looked forward to getting back to my daily three mile walks. It took a while, but I finally was able to make it that distance.

In January 2007, I decided that I would set a goal to complete a sprint triathlon within one year of being diagnosed. A sprint triathlon consists of swimming, biking, and running, but at much shorter distances than the Ironman mentioned in the previous chapter. I told my father about my plans, and a couple of days later, he called me back and asked if I would like him to do it with me. I thought that was a great idea and was excited about completing the triathlon with him.

For the next four months I spent several nights a week at the local gym. I walked several miles a night but could never really get back to running. At first, it just hurt my knees too much. Once my legs were stronger, I still was not able to run much farther than a quarter mile. As of the writing this chapter, it would still be very difficult for me to run a half mile. I am not quite sure why that is the case. I know that I am not in great shape, but I think it has more to do with what

I went through than anything else. I also began swimming in the pool and riding the stationary bike.

Once the weather improved, I was able to do my walking and biking outdoors. My first attempt at completing the triathlon came on May 19th in Galena, IL. I did not know it at the time that I registered, but Galena just happens to have one of the most difficult sprint triathlons in the country. This is due in part to the distances, which are a little longer than many sprint triathlons but the greatest factor is that the 17-mile bike ride is spent on very large hills. There is very little flat ground in the area. I was confident that I could finish because I had made sure that I could complete each distance more than a week before the event. However, I wasted too much energy early on and did not pace myself very well. I ended up dropping out during the bike section. My dad finished the race, and I was very proud of him. I was a little upset with myself because I knew that I could have made it if I had been a little more patient.

I could not give up. I had set my goal to finish one of these events prior to July 12th. We found out that Green Bay actually was holding their sprint triathlon on June 10th, so my father and I registered for that one. I continued training, and on June 10th I completed the Green Bay triathlon – almost two minutes ahead of my dad. Yes, I am bragging that I beat out a person twenty-eight years older than me.

The point of this section is not to tell you that you have to go out and compete in a triathlon, but to encourage you to set some realistic goals and to not give up until they are achieved. The training cost me a lot of time, energy, and some money, but it was worth it. Just knowing that I had reached my goal provided me with a great boost of confidence.

While driving to Green Bay on the day that I was diagnosed, I had told Casey that there was something that I really wanted to do one more time. I have spent a large part of my life playing basketball, and my favorite part of the game is dunking the ball. I told Casey that I really hoped I would get a chance to dunk again. Of course, this was nowhere near a top priority for me since I was more concerned with surviving. But I really hoped I would have the opportunity to do it again. As I began working out and training again, it was very difficult for me to jump because I had lost so much leg strength. It was not until about May that I could actually jump high enough to dunk, but I still had not done it in a game. Finally, God gave me that opportunity, too, and the timing could not have been more perfect. Exactly 52 weeks after the night that I told Casey that I would not wake up, I was playing at an open gym. During one of the games, I had the opportunity to dunk the ball, and I did. Instantly I remembered what I had told Casey in the car a year earlier. Once the game was over, I thanked the Lord for giving me the opportunity not only to fulfill one of my wishes, but just to be given a chance to play basketball again. It is not nearly as big a part of my life as it once was, but it was still a special moment for me to reflect on as I think about all I had gone through.

One other goal that I had was related to the triathlon. I wanted to be able to thank my doctor for all he had done for me. I had a picture taken of my dad and me after finishing the triathlon. I stopped at the hospital to give him a copy of the picture to show him that I was doing pretty well. He was very happy to hear and see that. I told him how much I appreciated all that he had done for me. Then I told him that I often tell people that God healed me and he used my doctor to do it. He told me that I wasn't quite right about that. He said, "God heals 'em. I just put the band-aids on."

My doctor's statement is probably a little bit too modest because he did so much more than put on a band-aid. He is an amazing doctor. Nevertheless, it sums up the point of this book. God is in charge, and He knows exactly what it is that we are going through at any time. He loves you more than you can know and desires for you to know Him and trust in Him.

This brings up the same question that has been asked several times so far. How can you believe in an all-powerful and loving God since the world is so full of death, disease, and suffering? Certainly, I cannot deny that these things exist.

After all, I did endure several months of leukemia and its treatments. So how can I defend my belief in the God of the Bible even though I suffered from cancer and know that many others have suffered and died from the disease? As you read the second section of this book, you will see that only the Bible provides an adequate answer to this important question.

The Future

My cancer diagnosis was a major event in my life and is one I hope never to have to deal with again. Nevertheless, I understand that there is always a chance for it to come back. From the literature I have read, those who survive my type of leukemia have a better than 90% success rate of it never returning. Those are great odds, but a relapse is certainly a possibility. Even if the leukemia does not come back, there are all sorts of difficulties and tragedies that could be in my future.

The reason that I am bringing this up is that I do not know what the future may hold for me. I am not promised tomorrow. I do not live in constant fear of what might happen to me, but instead, I focus on what it is that God expects from me right now. I have to admit that I do get a little nervous about looking at my feet after a walk because those little purple spots may show up again. However, if I allowed this worry or fear to consume me, then I would be completely ineffective in my service to God.

I am comforted by my beliefs that God is in control of all situations and, that no matter what happens to me, someday I will be in Heaven with Him.

I want to close this section of the book by mentioning the popular "Footprints in the Sand" poem. If a person can have the perspective that the character in the poem gains at the end, then he will be able to persevere through all of life's difficulties. While there have been a few different versions of the poem, here is the original, written by Mary Stevenson in 1936:

One night I dreamed I was walking along the beach with the Lord. Many scenes from my life flashed across the sky.

In each scene I noticed footprints in the sand. Sometimes there were two sets of footprints, other times there was one only.

This bothered me because I noticed that during the low periods of my life, when I was suffering from anguish, sorrow or defeat, I could see only one set of footprints, so I said to the Lord,

"You promised me, Lord, that if I followed you, you would walk with me always. But I have noticed that during the most trying periods of my life there has only been one set of footprints in the sand. Why, when I need you most, have you not been there for me?"

The Lord replied, "The years when you have seen only one set of footprints, my child, is when I carried you."

Life can be very difficult. At times, it may seem as if God is not near or is not listening. Do not believe it for a second. God is ever-present, and He knows when you are hurting. Those who earnestly seek Him will find Him, and He can bring comfort and hope to situations that seem hopeless. He gave me the strength, courage, perseverance, love, and support that I needed to survive my battle with cancer. Just like the person in the "Footprints" story, He has carried me through my difficult times. Nowhere was this more evident than the night that I told Casey I would not wake up in the morning. He can do the same for you, too, no matter how difficult your situation may be. I am eagerly looking forward to the time that I will be with Him in a place where there is no more suffering, sorrow, pain, bloodshed, or disease. I hope I will see you there, too.

Part Two:

Defense of the Biblical God

Chapter 8:

Does God Really Exist?

"For since the creation of the world God's invisible qualities – His eternal power and divine nature – have been clearly seen, being understood by the things that are made..."
- Romans 1:20

Introduction

People are often surprised to discover that the Bible does not make an effort to prove God's existence. Rather, it assumes that He does exist. In fact, the very first verse of the Bible tells us that God is the cause for the existence of everything else: "In the beginning God created the heavens and the earth" (Genesis 1: 1). This is not to say that the Bible never sets out to give evidence of God's existence, because there are places in which God provides examples to do just that. For example, in a lengthy discourse in Isaiah 40 – 46,

God shows that He is superior to all other gods, because He alone can foretell the future, and do it with amazing accuracy. In one of the prophecies in this section, God gave the name of the king (Cyrus) who would give the decree to send the Israelites back to their land after being exiled to Babylon for seventy years. The amazing part of this prophecy is that God named this king about a century and a half before Cyrus was even born!

Some well-meaning Christians have claimed that faith and reason are contradictory concepts. They believe that a person cannot learn about God through reason and research. Instead, belief in God is simply a matter of faith. As logical as this may seem, it does not line up well with what Scripture teaches on this subject. In reality, faith and reason do not contradict each other; they are complementary concepts. Reason and research can strengthen faith rather than mitigate against it.

In this chapter I want to help you examine the evidence for God's existence. To do this, we will examine three of the best-known arguments or philosophical "proofs" for God's existence. I will also examine one other "proof" that is often neglected by apologists. Rather than uncritically accepting them as evidence for the God of the Bible, I will show you that these proofs can only take a person so far. Also, we will see that some Christian apologists (people who defend the Christian faith) have made unwarranted jumps in their thinking and claimed that a particular argument proves the Bible. However, we will see that something else is needed to show a person that God – that is, the God of the Bible – is the only true God, and He does in fact exist.

Cause and Effect

The first philosophical argument for God's existence is known as the Cosmological Argument. This argument is based on the law of cause and effect. Essentially, it states that everything that has a beginning has a cause. All of science is based on this premise since the scientific method is based on the testing and repeatability of certain events. As the scientist observes an event, he attempts to determine what caused that particular reaction. Once he forms his hypothesis about this, he subjects his hypothesis to rigorous testing to see if his ideas can be verified. These tests rely on the law of cause and effect.

The Cosmological Argument argues from the existence of the present universe to a beginning of the universe and hence, a Beginner of the universe. It is possible to show that the universe had a beginning; however, many Christians have adopted a poor argument at this point. Many Christian apologists have latched on to the popular Big Bang theory of the origin of the universe. Most of the Big Bang models do posit a beginning to the universe many billions of years in the past. Yet this theory is constantly changing and is quite suspect, so it would be unwise for a Christian to use it with the Cosmological Argument to prove God's existence.[1]

Not only is it unwise to rely on the Big Bang, it is unnecessary. Einstein demonstrated that time is a physical property of matter. In other words, if matter exists, then time must exist and vice versa. As a result it is undeniable that the universe had a beginning, and since it had a beginning, then it must have had a cause. This is because matter could not have existed eternally, because if it did, then time would have had to exist for an infinite amount of time prior to today. Yet it is impossible to traverse an infinite amount of time to arrive at today's date.[2] Therefore, time must have had a beginning and hence, a Beginner. Christians believe this Beginner is the God of the Bible. This also nullifies the possibility of naturalistic (atheistic) evolution or any of the atheistic religions, such as Buddhism.

Someone might ask why this concept of time being a physical property of matter requires a beginner. Couldn't the universe have come into existence by itself? Could matter have made itself? Of course, these concepts are absurd. The idea of self-creation is impossible because something would have to be there in order to make itself. If the universe came into existence by itself, then this would go against every single observation we have ever made.[3] To believe this requires more faith than believing that someone or something made it. This is because we have never observed something make itself. All we have ever observed is that things that are made require a maker. To believe that the universe created itself would be a leap of blind faith; whereas, to believe that a Creator created the universe demonstrates a reasonable faith.

Critics of this argument often ask, "If everything has a beginning, and God made the universe, then who or what made God? This objection is based on a misunderstanding of the argument. The Cosmological Argument states that all things that have a beginning have a cause. The God of the Bible does not have a beginning because He is eternal. He does not need anyone to make Him because He has always been. In fact, it is interesting that when God spoke to Moses about freeing the Israelites, He told him that His name was I AM WHO I AM (Exodus 3:14). Many biblical scholars believe this refers to His self-existence and eternality. Later in the Bible, in the Book of Revelation, God is being praised in heaven as being the God "who was, and is, and is to come" (Revelation 4:8). The Bible teaches that God has always existed. He has always been; therefore, He does not need a cause.

The rationale behind the Cosmological Argument is sound. So, be that as it may, what does this argument reveal about the "Beginner"? First, it tells us that the Beginner is transcendent, meaning outside of the creation rather than part of it. This fact alone rules out the possibility of all the pantheistic religions such as Hinduism, the New Age Movement and most of the Eastern religions. These religions believe that "God is all" and "all is God." However, if this is true, then God would have to self-create, which, as we have seen, is a logical absurdity. Also, consider the remark made by Dash, the lightning-fast son of Mr. Incredible from *The Incredibles* movie. After hearing his mother claim that everyone was special, Dash retorted, "Which is another way of saying nobody is." In a sense he is right, and this applies to God as well. If everyone is God, then God is nothing special or out of the ordinary, so this belief is really quite meaningless.

Second, this argument reveals that the Beginner is all-powerful. Christians use the term omnipotent to refer to the idea of God being all-powerful. The Beginner must have had enough power to create the entire universe. The fact that He could create it not only shows His power; it also demonstrates His omniscience (all-knowledge). This portion of the argument cancels out all of the polytheistic religions in which many gods struggle against each other for power. An omnipotent and omniscient God has no rivals. The gods of polytheism do not have omnipotence or omniscience. Hence, none of them could have been the Beginner. Polytheism is not a valid option.

The form of the Cosmological Argument that has been discussed so far is known as the Kalam Cosmological Argument or Horizontal Cosmological Argument. There is another form of this argument known as the Vertical Cosmological Argument. This form of the argument demonstrates that the entire universe is currently dependent upon the Beginner for its existence. That is, not only did the Beginner "begin" the world, He continues to uphold or sustain it.[4] This fits very well with the biblical concept that Jesus Christ sustains "all things by His powerful word" (Hebrews 1:3) and that "in Him all things hold together" (Colossians 1:17).

Not only does this fit well with the biblical view of God, it also destroys another false view of God. Deism was a popular belief during the days of the so-called Enlightenment. It was an attempt to appease the secular view that miracles are not possible, but at the same time, appease the Christian view of a Creator. Basically, Deism states that God made the world but then backed away and let it run entirely according to the natural laws He put in place. The Deist's God is often called the Watchmaker God. Just like a watchmaker creates the watch and winds it to start working, the Deistic God started the world and then left it alone. The Deistic God cannot perform miracles because he cannot intervene in this world. However, the Vertical form of the Cosmological Argument completely refutes the concept that God is no longer involved in His creation. He is actively sustaining it. Deism also fails because it is self-contradictory. The deistic God cannot perform miracles in this world, but he has already done the most miraculous of all – the creation of the entire universe.

So far I have not proven the existence of the God of the Bible. The Cosmological Argument cannot do that by itself. It can only reveal certain aspects about the Beginner. He is all-powerful, all-knowing, transcendent, and is currently sustaining the universe. He is also monotheistic, meaning that there is only one God. Besides Christianity, other religions believe in a deity that fits this description, such as Judaism and Islam. Therefore, it is time to turn our attention to another argument to see if any other views can be weeded out.

Design and the Designer

The next major argument to be discussed is known as the Teleological Argument. This is also known as the "design argument" and has become very popular in recent years with the growth of the Intelligent Design Movement.[5] Briefly stated, this argument looks at the incredible complexity and seemingly purposeful design in the world and posits that only a Designer could have made such a world. Just as a building requires a builder, so too, does a designed universe require a Designer.

In the past few centuries, a popular example of this argument was William Paley's watchmaker argument. If a man found a watch on the ground, he would instantly know that it was not the product of chance random processes over billions of years. Because of its complexity and purpose, an intelligent being must have made it.

In the 1990s a stronger argument was promoted. Biochemist Michael Behe coined the phrase "irreducible complexity" in his highly successful book *Darwin's Black Box*. This term refers to creatures or structures that require several parts to be in operation at the same time and in the same place or it could not function. This argument has dealt a serious blow to naturalistic evolution. For his example, Behe talked about the mousetrap. It is a simple device with a few working parts. Nevertheless, all of those parts need to be in place at the right time and be made out of the right materials or the mousetrap would not function.

The universe displays mind-boggling complexity. Astronomers marvel over the extreme fine-tuning of the universe and our solar system. Biologists and chemists are amazed at the complexity of the human body and the wondrous inner workings of the cell. In each of these systems, any particular object depends upon the existence of numerous other objects. These things are millions of times more complex than a mousetrap, which is irreducibly complex. As such, the world must have had a Designer.

So what does the teleological argument reveal about the Designer? It tells us that He is incredibly intelligent and creative. Once again, polytheism is ruled out because its gods and goddesses are limited in intelligence and power. Only an all-powerful and all-knowing Designer designed the world with such amazing complexities, right?

Well, there is an objection to the teleological argument and it is one at which Christians need to take a serious look. Disteleology refers to certain things in this world which look like they are the product of a poor or cruel Designer. Why are there viruses and bacteria that kill millions of people each year? If the Designer was so great, why do our bodies run down? Why does the Designer allow cancer to kill or harm so many people each year? These questions cannot be answered satisfactorily by the Teleological Argument. More information is needed to provide a good answer to that question. This will be dealt with in the following two chapters. Nevertheless, design and purpose exist in this world. It strains credulity to think that one cell could come about by random chance processes. Someone or something had to have made it.

The Moral Argument

The final argument that I want to cover in this chapter is known as the Moral Argument. So far I have been able to narrow the identity of the Beginner and Designer to a mono-theistic God who is omnipotent, omniscient, transcendent, and eternal. The Moral Argument can take us a step further in our attempt to uncover the true identity of the Beginner.

The Moral Argument can be simply stated in four steps:

1) There is a universal moral law.
2) A universal law requires a universal Moral Law Giver.
3) The Moral Law Giver must be absolutely good.
4) Therefore, a universal Moral Law Giver exists.

There are some objections to these statements, but they can be answered easily. The most common objection is to the first point. Many will argue that there is not a universal moral law. However, when they do this, they are arguing that their view of morality (or immorality or amorality) is better. Thus, they are essentially using the moral law in an attempt to refute the moral law. Consider the following account from a discussion I had with one of my youth group students:

> A few years ago, we were discussing ethics and morality in youth group. We had a new girl in the group that night that began to debate me on every subject. She was arguing that all morality is relative (i.e. what is right for me may not be right for someone else, and what is wrong for me might not be wrong for someone else). We discussed several controversial subjects, and each topic elicited a similar response from the girl, "That might be true for you but not for somebody else." She argued with me on every topic. She even debated whether or not there were really three chairs next to me in the front of the room (for the record – there really were three chairs). She said, "Well, it might be three for you, but someone else might have a different reality." After debating about reality and morality for a while, I thought of taking a different approach. Rather than debate the peripheral subjects at hand, I wanted to get to the heart of her argumentation. She believed all morality and all truth is relative. I needed to show her that this is impossible. I stated, "Look, I KNOW there is a right and a wrong for every single person on this Earth." She instantly replied, "You can't know that!" To which I simply responded, "What did you say?" She started, "You can't know..." As she said the words, she slowed down and stopped because she realized that she was doing the very thing that she said cannot be done.

You see, in order to deny that moral absolutes exist, you have to propose a moral absolute – that moral absolutes are absolutely wrong. Everyone has a standard of right and wrong. It is true that some people view certain actions as being right whereas others see the same actions as being wrong. This is true even among Christians. Some believe any alcoholic use is sinful while others believe it can be done in moderation under certain circumstances. These types of examples are essentially dealing with one's convictions, not necessarily the moral law.

Once, a man was visiting a Sunday night Bible study at the church I was pastoring, and he started debating with me about the Ten Commandments. I said that they are the standards the God expects people to live up to.[6] Like the young lady in the previous example, he tried arguing that the Ten Commandments were relative. Other people might have other standards that are completely different. I wanted to get to the heart of the issue again, so I told him that they are absolutes from the Moral Law Giver and that my view of morality was better than his. He said that everyone gets to decide morality for himself. So once again I said that my morality was absolute and was better than his.[7] He said morality cannot be absolute and that all moral views are equally valid. I asked him if my view was equally valid, and he said that it was. So I reiterated that my equally valid view of morality is that the biblical position on morality was superior to all others. He continued to argue that this was impossible because all morality is relative. Finally, I asked him if his position on this subject was better than mine. He said that it was. I pointed out that by making this claim, he was confirming the Moral Law and was saying that his answer contradicted his claim that all morality is relative and equally valid. You see, he was claiming that his relativistic view of morality was better than an absolute view. By claiming this, he was contradicting his belief that all views are equally valid, and he was setting his view up as morally superior. Rather than refuting the Moral Law, this man actually used it in an attempt to refute it.

C.S. Lewis promoted the most popular version of this argument. In *Mere Christianity*, he wrote at length concerning this argument and stated the following about his time as an atheist:

> Just how had I got this idea of *just* and *unjust?* A man does not call a line crooked unless he has some idea of a straight line. What was I comparing this universe with when I called it unjust. . . . Of course I could have given up my idea of justice by saying it was nothing but a private idea of my own. But if I did that, then my argument against God collapsed too—for the argument depended on saying that the world was really unjust, not simply that it did not happen to please my private fancies. Thus in the very act of trying to prove that God did not exist—in other words, that the whole of reality was senseless—I found I was forced to assume that one part of reality—namely my idea of justice—was full of sense.[8]

Just like the two examples that I cited, Lewis' story demonstrates that one cannot attempt to refute the Moral Argument without using it. This means that the Moral Argument is undeniably true.

So what does all of this tell us about the Moral Law Giver, whom we call God? First, since He is the standard of what is morally good, then He must be absolutely good. Second, this argument does away with the Islamic god. They believe that Allah is unknowable and unlimited. The fact that the Moral Argument reveals some of God's morality reveals that He is not entirely unknowable. Also, the fact that He serves as the absolute standard of morality shows that His morality does not change. Muslims believe it is possible for their god to change his mind about things. He could send someone to hell simply because he did not like them – even if that person was faithful to follow all of Islam's teachings. They believe that he cannot be held to a certain standard because he is unlimited. However, the Moral Argument reveals a knowable God whose standards do not change.

Transcendental Argument

The final argument for God's existence that I want to explain is often neglected by Christian apologists. It is called the Transcendental Argument for God, or TAG for short. By itself, the argument is powerful enough to demolish almost every other philosophy and belief system. When combined with the three arguments already covered, it makes an extremely compelling case for the God of the Bible.

This view forces a person to examine their own starting points (presuppositions) to see if their own view is consistent. A common way of stating this is that the Transcendental Argument defends Christianity by demonstrating the impossibility of the contrary. In other words, Christianity must be true because all of the other views are impossible.

In my first book, my co-author provided an example of how this argument could be used in dealing with a person who did not believe in God. This person thought Christianity was "unscientific" because it proposes that God made everything, and, according to this hypothetical person, science can only reach naturalistic conclusions. First, instead of accepting the unbeliever's notion that Christianity is "unscientific" we would challenge it. This can be done by pointing out that science is only possible if there is a God who created the world to follow natural laws, and created us with minds that could discover and understand these laws.

The second step in this argument is to show that the unbeliever's position is inconsistent. In this particular case, we would show that a person who holds to philosophical naturalism (nature is all there is) has no basis for believing in scientific laws. After all, if the universe and everything in it came about by random chance processes, then there is no reason to think that scientific laws should exist at all. Worse yet, there is no reason for him to trust his own thinking, because his brain is nothing but a collection of chemicals that randomly came together at just the right time and place.

As if that still is not bad enough, he could not justify having a free will to argue for or against his position or mine. Since his brain (and the rest of his body) is just a collection of chemicals, then we really have no free will. He has to believe what he does because that is the way he is made, and I have to believe what I do because that is how the chemicals that I am made of have determined I would think. If this were the case, there would be no reason to try to convince or persuade a person of anything.

Not only does the philosophical naturalist think inconsistently, he also lives inconsistently. Many of them do try to persuade or convince people to hold to their line of thinking. When they do this, they are, according to the logical extension of their own view, trying to convince someone to believe contrary to what they have to believe. Moreover, they are also utilizing the moral argument discussed earlier because they apparently believe their view is superior to others.

This argument can be used against other belief systems as well. There are some Christians who would question whether or not this proves the God of the Bible. Even if it does not provide absolute proof for God's existence, it is another powerful line of reasoning which leads to the conclusion that God exists.

Conclusion

Without using the Bible, it is possible to discover that a God exists Who is the Beginner, Designer, and Moral Law Giver. This God is omnipotent, omniscient, creative, good, transcendent, and yet immanent.[9] It is also possible to show that none of the other views can be held consistently. Many Christians believe that these arguments prove the existence of the God of the Bible. While they are definitely a good start, there is a serious issue that must be addressed. Namely, how can one believe in an all-powerful and loving Designer when so many bad things exist in the world?

Chapter 9:

The Problem of Evil and the Unsuccessful Attempts to Answer It

"Where is the wise man? Where is the scholar?
Where is the philosopher of this age? Has not God made
foolish the wisdom of the world?"
- 1 Corinthians 1:20

Introduction

In the previous chapter I demonstrated that it is possible to prove the existence of an all-powerful Creator through philosophical arguments. However, these arguments fail to provide answers to some of life's greatest questions, such as why an all-loving and all-powerful God would allow death and suffering to occur. This objection is typically known as the problem of evil. So, by themselves, these arguments are not conclusive. There are reasonable answers to these difficult questions, but they cannot be solved by man's wisdom. The only sensible and satisfying answers to these great dilemmas come from the Bible.

Before I show you the answers to these tough questions from the Bible, I want you to see that the other religions and philosophies cannot provide any hope in addressing the question of the problem of evil. For the rest of this chapter, I am going to show how some of the other major religions and belief systems attempt to deal with the problem of evil. By the time we are done, you will see that they fail in their efforts to deal with this issue. In the final chapter, I will present the biblical answer to this objection and defend it.

As you read through this section, please notice the major differences between these views. It has become a popular notion in our culture to assume that all religions are basically the same, but nothing could be further from the truth. Not only are they far different in their practices, but their beliefs about the nature of God are vastly different. How then can they all be the same? Either they are all wrong or one is right and the rest are wrong. Two or more contradicting views cannot be right.

Atheism and the Problem of Evil

Atheism is not typically classified as a religion, but it is a philosophical system that says there is no God. Some atheists, known as hard atheists, make the bold claim that there is no God. The others, known as soft atheists, are not quite as bold. They say that they believe there is no God. Either way, it is a system that claims that no God exists, or, even if He does, He is irrelevant.

Atheism is an interesting belief system because it is based not so much on what it believes, but on what it sees as the failure(s) of other belief systems. The two most common arguments for atheism are the belief in evolution and the problem of evil. As will be shown, neither of these arguments can prove the atheist's system. Nor can atheism answer the problem of evil.

First, the atheist's belief in evolution does not disprove the existence of a god. It is entirely possible to conceive of a god who made all things by the process of evolution. In fact, many people claim to believe this very thing. They are known as theistic evolutionists. Their beliefs do not fit the description of the biblical God who made all things over the course of six days and made Adam from the dust of the ground and Eve from one of Adam's ribs. Humanity did not ascend through some sort of evolutionary scheme from ape-like creatures to man. Nevertheless, even if evolution were true – which I strongly reject – it does not prove that atheism is true.

Second, atheists often present the problem of evil as support for their view. They argue that there cannot be a God of love because so much evil exists in the world. This sounds like a strong argument at first, but it has serious flaws. The greatest problem with this argument is that the atheist has no standard by which he can say something is good or evil. After all, if the atheist is correct, then this world is simply the product of random chance processes that have occurred over billions of years. There is no right or wrong, good or evil. There is just matter, which is neither good nor evil in and of itself. It just is. How can the atheist accuse God of allowing evil in a world in which evil cannot exist or be defined?

As was shown in the previous chapter, a person has to use the Moral Argument when trying to refute it. This is exactly what the atheist does with the problem of evil. They determine that something is evil or wrong, such as a child dying of a terrible disease. Next, they claim that God would never allow this and, if He did allow it, then He would cure the child. If He did not cure the child, then He must not be good. If He could not cure the child, then He must not be all-powerful. This is the atheist's argument. While they are correct that a child dying from an awful disease is a terrible thing, they cannot claim that it is evil. After all, if morality is decided by the individual or the society, then an individual or society could decide that it would be good for these things to happen. Hitler's Germany decided that it would be best to kill all of the Jews. While most people rightly find this thinking revolting, the atheist really cannot consistently say that Hitler was wrong.

Ultimately, the atheist cannot answer the problem of evil. For them, the "bad" things exist because that is how they evolved. There truly is no good or bad because morality can only be decided by the individual or culture. Therefore, morality is relative, and what may be seen as evil one day could be seen as good the next.

Finally, the atheist is guilty of faulty logic. They believe that the problem of evil argues against the existence of God. However, an absolute Moral Law Giver (God) must exist for anyone to claim that something is good or evil. Hence, the atheist's argument is self-defeating.

Many atheists have either become or else claim to be agnostics. This term refers to someone who claims that it is impossible for anyone to have certain knowledge of God or certain knowledge of reality. It is full-blown skepticism. Agnostics reject Christianity because Christians claim to know God and know about God, both of which are impossible from their skeptical perspective. Not only is knowledge about God impossible but so is absolute knowledge of reality. For the agnostic, if God exists, He is irrelevant. I often wonder why agnostics are not skeptical of their skepticism.

Like atheists, agnostics often utilize the problem of evil as a charge against the biblical concept of God. However, also like the atheist, the agnostic has no basis for making such a claim. First, it is impossible for the agnostic to know whether or not evil really exists since it must necessarily be part of the unknowable reality. Second, even if evil could be recognized, it cannot be used as an argument against God because this would require the use of the Moral Law to determine what it is. And if the Moral Law is used, then there must be a Moral Law Giver. Like the atheist's argument, the agnostic's claim is self-refuting.

Agnosticism is also self-defeating. They claim that if God exists, then He is unknowable and irrelevant because it is impossible to know anything about God. However, in making this statement, they are revealing something about God – that He is unknowable. It is absurd to say that nothing can be known about God and at the same time say something about Him. Agnostics typically make the same claim about reality – that it cannot be known for sure. I wonder how they know enough about unknowable reality to say that it cannot be known.

The Eastern Religions and the Problem of Evil

Hinduism is one of the largest and oldest religions in the world. It dates back to the third millennium B.C., soon after the Tower of Babel incident recorded in the Bible. Many, if not all, of the Eastern mystical religions (Buddhism, Taoism, Shintaoism, Confucianism, etc.) find their roots in Hinduism. At the heart of this belief system is a concept called karma. This idea basically says that whatever an individual (whether person or creature) sows, he or she will reap. If a person is good in this life, then he will have a better life once he is reincarnated in the next life. On the other hand, if a person does evil in this life, then he will have evil done to him in the next.

As a Christian I completely reject the notion of reincarnation. The Bible says that a person will face judgment when this life is over. There are no second chances once a person dies (Hebrews 9:27). But what about the problem of evil? Can Hinduism or these other religions offer a satisfying answer? The answer is an emphatic "No!" In fact, they require the existence of evil.

The "law" of karma shows that evil will always exist and as such, there is no hope in ever overcoming evil. Perhaps an individual can escape from the cycle of reincarnation and achieve nirvana, but the world, as a whole, never can. This is because whatever a person reaps, he must also sow. Since there are people who do evil things in this world today, then there must be people in the next life who will perform evil actions to these people who must reap evil. Then, the person who did evil (to repay the other man's evil in his previous life) must have evil done to him in the next life. This must continue for eternity or the law of karma is no law at all. Hinduism cannot solve the problem of evil.

Buddhism has perhaps the worst answer of all when it comes to suffering and evil. For the Buddhist, all pain and suffering is merely an illusion.[1] So for those poor individuals suffering from a cancer diagnosis, Buddhism would teach them that this entire physical realm is nothing but an illusion. There is no such thing as pain or sickness. It's all in a person's mind. They will never be truly enlightened until they realize that their suffering is not real.

This is a horrible thing to say to someone who has lost a loved one, is currently watching a loved one suffer from cancer, or who is personally suffering from cancer. While a person may be able to deceive himself by believing that he does not have cancer when he really does, he might still die by the cancer whether he believes it to be an illusion or not. The cancer that nearly took my life was no illusion. It showed up on numerous tests, and it had a dramatic effect on my body before I ever had any idea that it was there.

Buddhism can offer no hope for answering the problem of evil, either.

Many other Eastern philosophies believe in universal dualism. This is often symbolized by the popular yin yang, the circular black and white symbol commonly seen on martial arts' material. Essentially, this concept states that good and evil (or light and darkness) are two sides of the same coin. They are equal and opposite forces that are dependent upon each other for their own existence.

The problem with this view should be readily apparent. If good is dependent upon evil for its existence then evil must always exist if there is to be good in the world. Thus, there is no hope of ever overcoming evil. As long as one hopes that good will exist, then evil must be there as well.

Islam and the Problem of Evil

Although it is monotheistic, Islam cannot adequately address the problem of evil, either. It teaches that everything that has ever happened or will ever happen occurs because Allah has willed it. All of the diseases, rapes, murders and every other awful event in this world have happened because Allah willed that it would. Their god wants these things to happen. Although they may provide reasons for why their god would will these things, many Islamic apologists would not argue with this point at all.

In other words, if a person is dying of cancer then the Muslim must conclude that this is happening because Allah wanted it to happen. Since their god is responsible for all the good and all the evil that has ever happened, it is impossible to have any confidence that evil will ever be done away with.

At this point, someone may ask if this is any different than the biblical teaching on this subject. It certainly is. I will spend the next chapter addressing this extremely important distinction. Although many have been led to believe that Allah and the God of the Bible are the same, they are very different. For example, Islam emphatically teaches that Allah has no son. In fact, they consider it blasphemous to make that claim. They also reject the idea that Jesus died on a cross for the sins of mankind. Christianity, on the other hand, is based on the idea that Jesus Christ is the Son of God and that He died for our sins.

Mormonism and the Problem of Evil

Mormonism is the common name for what is officially called The Church of Jesus Christ of Latter Day Saints. Sometimes this title is abbreviated as LDS. Many people have been led to believe that Mormonism is just another Christian denomination. This is false. While I could spend entire chapters on this subject, their view of the problem of evil is enough to show that it is not a Christian denomination.[2]

As will be demonstrated in the next chapter, the Bible teaches that death and suffering entered the world as a result of Adam's sin. This is known as the Fall of man. Mormonism turns this teaching around completely. Rather than the Fall being the worst event in the history of the world, the founders of Mormonism praised Adam for choosing to eat the fruit. For them, the Fall was one of the greatest things that has ever happened.

Mormons claim to believe in four holy books: the King James Version of the Bible, *The Book of Mormon*, *Doctrine and Covenants*, and *The Pearl of Great Price*. Following are quotes from the latter three books indicating the Mormon view of Adam's sinful choice.

2 Nephi 2:25 (*Book of Mormon*) states, "Adam fell that men might be; and men are, that they might have joy." Paragraph 65 of *Doctrine and Covenants* states, "Adam deliberately and wisely chose (to touch the forbidden tree) and partook of the fruit." Moses 5:10-11 (*Pearl of Great Price*) states, "Adam cried, 'Because of my transgression my eyes are opened, and in this life I shall have joy." Finally the Mormon Catechism proclaims, "We ought to consider

the fall of our first parents as one of the great steps to eternal exaltation and happiness."

Why do Mormons believe that the cause of death and suffering was a wonderful event? Because, for them, it is "one of the great steps to eternal exaltation and happiness." You see, Mormon theology teaches that Mormon men have the opportunity to achieve godhood by living an exemplary life according to their religion's standards. The only way that they could ever prove themselves worthy of this honor is if Adam ate the fruit.

At this point, one must wonder if Mormonism teaches that evil will ever be overcome. The answer is that it is impossible to know. Perhaps the evil on Earth will stop one day, but for Mormons who achieve godhood, the possibility (or perhaps necessity) of evil will always exist in the world(s) that they hope to rule. Thus, Mormonism cannot provide a satisfactory answer to the problem of evil.

Conclusion

It would be impossible in the space of this book to cover every single world religion to see how they fail to address the problem of evil. Nevertheless, the above sampling represents a huge percentage of non-Christian people in this world. There is much more that could be said about each of these religions and/or philosophies, but this chapter has enough information to show how they fail to address this crucial question. The final chapter of this book is designed to show you why biblical Christianity is the only belief system that can adequately address this issue.

Chapter 10:

Biblical Christianity – The Only Solution to the Problem of Evil

And I heard a loud voice from the throne saying, "Now the dwelling of God is with men, and He will live with them. They will be His people, and God Himself will be with them and be their God. He will wipe every tear from their eyes. There will be no more death or mourning or crying or pain, for the old order of things has passed away."
- Revelation 21:3-4

Introduction

I have made some bold claims for Christianity and the God of the Bible throughout this book without taking the time to try to prove them. This final chapter is designed to address some of these claims to show that they are not baseless. Instead, they are well-reasoned and thoroughly defensible positions. More importantly, they are true. Not because I have said so, but because they are based on the word of God, and God cannot lie (Hebrews 6:18).

Defining Biblical Christianity

Before I get to these answers, it is necessary to define what I mean by the term "biblical Christianity." It might seem strange to require a definition for this, because one would think that it is rather straightforward. However, many groups have taken the name "Christian" yet believe very little of the Bible. "Biblical Christianity" is a term that refers to all those who accept that the Bible is the literal word of God and is authoritative in every area. Biblical Christians accept the biblical teachings of the full inspiration of Scripture, the literal six day creation account in Genesis, the virgin birth, deity, death, burial, bodily resurrection, and future physical return of Jesus Christ. There is some difference of opinion among biblical Christians on how certain biblical teachings should be understood, but they still affirm the truth of these teachings.

Christianity and the Origin of Evil

If we are to understand the biblical solution to the problem of evil, then we need to know what the Bible teaches about the origin of evil. The Bible reveals that God created a perfect world. After each of the first five days of the creation week, God declared that what He had made was "good." Following the sixth day when God created the land animals and man, God declared that everything He had made was "very good" (Genesis 1:31).

The Bible confirms this in other ways as well. For example, on the sixth day, the Bible reveals that all of the land animals and birds were originally created as vegetarians (Genesis 1:30). Man was also created as a vegetarian (Genesis 1:29). It was not until after the worldwide flood of Noah's day that God told man that he could eat animals (Genesis 9:3). Prior to the Fall of man, there were no thorns or thistles and no death or suffering in the world, either. God created a perfect world, but it is no longer that way. Something happened.

Some time after the sixth day but before Genesis chapter 3, one of the angels, named Lucifer, decided that he wanted to be like God. The fourteenth chapter of Isaiah indicates that this angel's pride played a part in his rebellion against God. Soon after that, Lucifer (also called Satan) went to the Garden of Eden in an effort to deceive Eve (Genesis 3). Speaking through a serpent, he was able to get Eve to question God's command about the one fruit tree in the Garden from which they were not allowed to eat. Eve fell for his trap, took the fruit, and ate it. She also gave it to Adam, and he ate the fruit. They instantly realized that they had done something terribly wrong, and for the first time in their lives they felt shame and guilt.

God had already told Adam that if he violated the command concerning this fruit, then Adam would die. Oftentimes, people question why Adam did not die physically on that day. In a sense, he did. The actual Hebrew phrase used here indicates that Adam was going to start to die and he would continue to die until he was dead. This is exactly what happened.

Many people have thought that death was an extreme punishment for such a sin. After all, Adam and Eve only ate a fruit, right? Wrong! There was nothing inherently magical about that tree. The problem was that Adam and Eve essentially made the decision that they wanted to live by their own rules rather than the rules of their Creator. Not only that, although some have thought of this as a "small sin," we have to keep in mind that all sin is a violation of the law set forth by an infinitely holy God. Therefore, all sin carries with it an infinite punishment.

There is another aspect to this that needs to be examined. In a sense, death was a gracious penalty for mankind. If Adam and Eve had not eaten the fruit, they would have lived forever in a perfect world. However, once they ate the fruit, Adam and Eve would live in a sin-cursed world. Can you even imagine how dreadful it would be to live forever in a world like ours? We try to run from death and many people spend their entire lives trying to fight it. However, at some point we have to realize that eternal life on this planet would truly be a miserable existence because there is so much evil and suffering, which would only be multiplied many times over if all the wicked people throughout history were still alive.

Not only did their sin bring physical death, it also brought about a break in man's relationship with God. Although Adam was still able to communicate with God, it was not the same as before. Adam was afraid to stand before his Maker because of the shame that he felt for his sin. For the first time, Adam was separated from his Creator. Many theologians choose to call this separation "spiritual death."

In addition to losing perfect fellowship with the Lord, Adam's disobedience would also introduce more problems for the world. In Genesis chapter 3, God revealed that there would be a curse on the animal kingdom, man and woman, and the ground itself.[1] Romans 8:22 supports this by stating that the whole creation is groaning as a result of Adam's sin. In the midst of the pronouncement of the Curse, God also provided the first promise of the Messiah in Genesis 3:15.

Death and suffering entered the world because of man's sin. The way that things are now is not the way God made the world, and He did not mess it up. The reason that cancer, death, suffering, and so many other horrible things occur in our world is because we wrecked it.

Is God Responsible for Sin?

Many of my students have questioned why God would even place the tree of the knowledge of good and evil in the Garden in the first place. Why even give Adam and Eve an opportunity to sin? My response is that God wanted people to love and obey Him because they wanted to love and obey Him. If God did not provide an opportunity for man to disobey, then man could not truly ever demonstrate obedience from a willing heart. He would have no choice but to obey. If Adam and Eve did not have a choice, then they would have been like robots in that they would not have an option to disobey. Since God gave them a choice, then He is absolved from being the author of sin and suffering. It is man's fault.

Another question that often comes up is whether or not God is still to blame because He knew Adam and Eve would sin and yet He still created them. The Bible does teach that God knew that they would sin, but this does not mean that God is to blame. There are two issues that need to be discussed here. First, since God gave Adam and Eve the freedom to choose to obey Him or disobey Him, Adam and Eve must bear the responsibility for their failure. For example, we do not hold parents responsible for the failures of their grown children. If a man's son commits a crime as an adult, we do not hold the man responsible for that crime. We might be tempted to question his skills as a parent, but we recognize that the son made his own choices and must face the consequences of his crime. Second, when a couple decides to have a child, they understand that their child is going to make mistakes and sin. Yet they still choose to have that child. For them, the love that they will have for that child and the love they might receive in return from that child make it worth the trouble.

In the same way, God is not held responsible for the sins of Adam and Eve. God created the potential for them to sin, but it was their choice to disobey. In philosophical terms, we would say that they actualized that potential. Also, it is my belief that God felt that it was worth it to create us even though He knew that billions of people throughout history would reject Him. Those that have trusted in Him make humanity worth the trouble.[2]

Importance of Proper Perspective

Having this perspective made things quite a bit easier for me in the hospital or any other difficult situation in which I have found myself. I often pondered this while I was in the hospital. You see, one of the reasons that I had complete confidence in God during my ordeal is that I knew beyond any shadow of a doubt that God is good.

Many Christians and unbelievers struggle with this concept. They doubt whether or not God is absolutely good. The main reason for this is that they do not have a proper perspective on this issue. They have bought into secular thinking which proclaims that death and suffering have been around for millions and billions of years before Adam and Eve arrived on the scene. They might still believe that God created everything, but they accept the popular notion that the Earth is billions of years old. If these things are accepted as true, then it is difficult to believe the rest of the Bible. After all, if God cannot get His story straight in the first few chapters, then why should a person trust Him in the rest of the Bible?

Sadly, too many Christians have been led to believe that this issue just is not very important. However, when it comes to the issue of death and suffering, it is extremely important. Consider this for a moment. If God did create everything over the course of billions of years, then most of the fossil record provides evidence of many of the life forms that have existed over that time span. Yet these fossils contain evidence of destruction. First, many of these fossils are remains of dead animals. Some of these remains reveal that the bones were damaged by teeth or claws. Second, scientists have found evidence of terrible diseases in the fossil record – supposedly before Adam and Eve ever lived. These include arthritis and cancer. That's right! The fossil record contains evidence of cancer – even in dinosaur bones. So what does this have to do with God? Think about it. If cancer existed before Adam and Eve, which is what the old-earth view of the fossil record teaches, then God is responsible for cancer and every other disease. He would be the cause of the suffering and death found in the fossil record.

Can you imagine how difficult it would be to completely rely on God's faithfulness and goodness while dealing with a cancer diagnosis if a person accepts this view of things? After all, if God is responsible for cancer, and it was around long before Adam and Eve, then it must have been part of the world that God declared was "very good." This means that God must think cancer is very good. For me, this would have meant that the disease that nearly took my life and has taken the lives of millions around the world is a very good thing according to God. Would it even be possible for me to think of God as good if He liked the disease that was killing me? This is not the God of love revealed in the Bible. No, the God of the Bible views death as an enemy that will one day be destroyed (1 Corinthians 15:26).

If Christians would take God at His word, then they would realize that death and suffering came into the world as a result of Adam's sin. There is no good reason to accept man's opinions that the Earth is billions of years old and that death and suffering were around before Adam.[3] Instead, since death and suffering are man's fault, then there was no reason to blame God for the condition I was in. I understood that I was a sinner who deserved to die. As a result, there was one common question that I never asked during my battle with leukemia – Why me? I never asked "Why me?" because I knew exactly why. The real questions for me were "Why did it take so long?" and "Why not everyone else?" I knew that if my life was taken, it would not be unjust. As a sinner, I deserve to suffer and die because I have rebelled against my Creator. He would be perfectly just for taking me out of this world, yet He continues to shower His love, grace, and mercy on me by allowing me to live and to use me in His service.

In an earlier chapter I mentioned that it was so important to have the right mindset when facing difficult times. It is even more important to have a proper view of God and a proper view of yourself. When you realize that God is perfect and that we are not, then it is easy to understand why He is not to blame for the difficult situations in which we so often find ourselves.

The Only Solution to the Problem of Evil

The biblical perspective on death and suffering does not end here. Not only is God not to be blamed for evil, but He provided a solution to it. The Bible reveals that at the time of the Curse, God also provided hope that one day evil would be overcome. In Genesis 3:15 God stated the "seed" of the woman" (one of her future descendants) would one day crush the head of the serpent (Satan). In the process this "seed" would bruise His heel. This may seem strange at first, especially if this is the first time you have ever read or heard this. However, as you become familiar with the rest of Scripture, you realize how this verse came true in a very literal way.

Four thousand years after the serpent deceived Eve and led mankind in rebellion, the Creator stepped into this world to conquer His enemy. It is interesting that God revealed that the "seed" would be of the woman. Every other time the term "seed" is used in this manner in the Bible it is attributed to a man. This is remarkable because when the Creator stepped into His creation, He came as the "seed" of the woman. This occurred when Jesus was conceived by the Holy Spirit in Mary's womb. Since she was a virgin when Jesus was conceived, He could accurately be called the "seed" of the woman rather than of a man.

Many readers are familiar with the Christmas story. However, it is at the other end of Christ's earthly life that we see the fulfillment of the other promise made in Genesis 3:15. More than three decades later, Jesus was hanging on a cross outside of Jerusalem with nails piercing His wrists and one spike nailed through his feet. Of course, readers are probably familiar with the crucifixion of Jesus. However, many are not aware of the manner in which God's promise back in the Garden would be literally fulfilled. As a crucifixion victim, Christ would have literally bruised one of His heels. This is a natural result of crucifixion. As the crucifixion victim fights for air, he is forced to push himself upward so that he can take in a full breath. To do this, he must push his weight upward with his legs. However, because of the position in which the spike is driven through both feet, one of the victim's heels is pushed hard into the upright beam of the cross. As the victim repeatedly clamors for air, his heel is literally bruised against the cross. While this is extremely interesting and provides evidence for the supernatural origin of the Bible, it is not the most important part of the promise found in Genesis 3:15.

After Jesus died on the cross He was laid in a tomb. Three days later, He rose from the dead and began to appear to His followers. In the process of conquering death, the Creator also conquered the serpent. The Resurrection demonstrated Christ's power over the grave and guaranteed Satan's doom.

The best part about all of this is that Christ has offered all of us a chance to take part in His victory over evil. One of the most famous Bible verses perfectly summarizes this message: "For God so loved the world that He gave His one and only Son, that whoever believes in Him shall not perish but have eternal life" (John 3:16). The Creator entered this world so that He could die the death that each one of us deserves. He rose from the dead and offered to save everyone who would trust in Him alone for their salvation. Each of us deserves to die for our own sins. Graciously, Christ was willing to take the punishment for us and is willing to forgive any and all who would believe in Him. Romans 10:9-10 states, "That if you confess with your mouth, 'Jesus is Lord,' and believe in your heart that God raised Him from the dead, you will be saved. For it is with your heart that you believe and are justified, and it is with your mouth that you confess and are saved." Salvation cannot be earned by our good works. It is a gift from God that can only be accepted by faith.

It is also important to point out that this is the only way a person can be saved from their sins. It has become increasingly popular in our day and age to hear people, even some pastors, say that Jesus is just one of the many ways to God. Jesus flatly denied this when He said, "I am the way and the truth and the life. No one comes to the Father except through Me" (John 14:6). Not only did He explicitly teach this, it is also implicitly taught in the Bible. On the night that He was arrested, Jesus prayed that if it were possible to save sinners in any other way (other than the crucifixion) then let that be done. Nevertheless, He prayed the famous words, "Not My will, but Thine, be done" (Luke 22:42, KJV). If a person could get to heaven through another means, then Christ would not have gone to the cross. The fact that God raised Him from the dead demonstrates that He confirmed Christ's message.[4] As such, Jesus is the only way to the Father.

At this point, I need to show you that the Bible also predicts an end to the evil and suffering in the world. At some point in the future, possibly the very near future, the Creator is going to return to this world. One day He will judge this world. For those who have rejected Him, Jesus is going to give them what they think they want – a life without Him. What these people fail to realize is that this life without

Him will be for all eternity, and it will be the worst sort of life imaginable. There will be no more love, joy, or peace. These people will spend eternity suffering for their own sins because they refused to humble themselves and ask Christ to take away their sins. As a result, they will suffer for their own sins for all eternity in the lake of fire (Rev. 20:15).

On the other hand, all of those who have trusted in Christ for their salvation will enjoy eternal life with their Creator. They will dwell in a place where there will never be any sorrow, suffering, pain, disease, bloodshed, or death. None of the people who are there will be deserving of this blissful existence. They did not earn their spot in heaven. It was paid for by the Creator on the cross two thousand years ago.

Perhaps I could summarize it this way: The Creator made a perfect world. We messed everything up with our sin. The Creator stepped into our world and offered us the way to dwell with Him for all eternity. He promised to wipe every tear from our eyes. If you think you can imagine how wonderful all of this will be, consider these words from the Apostle Paul, "No eye has seen, no ear has heard, no mind has conceived what God has prepared for those who love Him" (1 Corinthians 2:9). We cannot even begin to imagine how great eternal life with the Creator will be, because no matter how great we think it will be, it will be far better.

Conclusion

We have reached the end of our brief look at the problem of evil. I have shown you that the various religions and philosophies of the world cannot adequately deal with this issue. In fact, some of them cannot even claim that there is such a thing as evil. Christianity is the only belief system that can adequately explain why evil exists.

More importantly, the God of the Bible has also promised to do away with evil once and for all and has invited all of us to spend eternity with Him. Would you accept that invitation if you have not already done so? If you would like to become a follower of Jesus Christ then think seriously about the following truths:

- You are a sinner that has repeatedly broken God's commands. If you doubt this, just compare your life with the Ten Commandments, and see if you have lived up to them. (see Romans 3:23)
- Now that you realize you are a sinner, you need to understand that you cannot save yourself. You need a Savior because what you really deserve is death. (see Romans 6:23)
- Jesus Christ is the only Person worthy of being the Savior because He lived a sinless life and is also the Judge. He did not need to die for His own sins.

Instead, He died for your sins and mine. (see John
3:16 and 2 Corinthians 5:21)

- The Bible talks about repentance in connection with
salvation. Repentance refers to a willful commitment
to turn from your life of sin to a life of serving the
Savior. (see Acts 3:19 and 17:30)

- After considering these truths, ask God to save you.
There is no magic formula of what to say. Simply
pour out your heart to God. As you pray, you should
confess that you recognize your own sinfulness and
your need for Him to save you. He promises to save
all who call on Him.

- If you have just done this, I would like to congratu-
late you on joining the family of God. Romans 8:14-
17 reveals that you are now a child of God.

- Also, if you have just done this, would you consider
sending me an email and letting me know. I would
love to be able to pray for you, and it would be an
encouragement to know that God used this book to
lead you to Him. I cannot take credit for what you
have just done because our Creator has done it all.

- Find a church that faithfully preaches and teaches
the Word of God. Many churches do not do this, so
be careful in choosing a church. It might be helpful
to simply ask the pastor whether or not the church

believes what was mentioned in this chapter (i.e. that God created a perfect world about 6,000 years ago, that Adam and Eve brought sin and death into the world by eating the forbidden fruit, and that Christ was born of a virgin and literally rose from the dead). If the church affirms these things, then it will likely take God's Word seriously in other areas.

- Get yourself a Bible and begin reading and studying it. Ask God to guide and teach you as you read. Continue to spend time every day with Him in prayer. You will be amazed at the changes He will make in your life.

Appendix A:

A Wife's Perspective

A s I told people about this book project, I repeatedly heard that I needed to have Casey write some thoughts. I asked her if she would be willing to do it and thankfully she agreed. After all, it is not only the patient that suffers during a cancer diagnosis; the family does, too. I hope that you will find comfort and hope in the following words from my wonderful wife who stood by me every step of the way.

Casey's Thoughts

I am not really the writer in the family, but many people have asked to hear my side of the story. I can't really put into words what went through my mind when we heard the phrase that would change our lives forever: "You have leukemia." Tim is the ultimate optimist while I am, as Tim says, the ultimate pessimist (although I like to say I am just the realist). So we tend to balance each other out quite nicely. While Tim was wondering when he would be able to get back to teaching, I was torn by so many different emotions. Not knowing what the future holds can be a very scary thing. Everyone knows that tragedy can strike at any moment, but it's so easy to forget while going about our busy lives every day.

I have always wanted to be a wife and mother. Having a stay-at-home mom while growing up gave me such a desire to do the same for my children. After the diagnosis, I had to think about a future that I never thought I would have to – one without Tim. Tim is the provider of our family. I have worked a few jobs now and then when necessary, but my primary role has been wife and mother. Now I had to think about becoming a single parent and sole provider. I am very blessed to have many people in my life who I know I could count on to help take care of us, but I wasn't sure how I would provide financially for myself and my two children.

The first person that I called was my sister. I could not even get the words out of my mouth. All I could say was "Tim has…Tim has…." Tim is the love of my life and my best friend. Even after twelve years of marriage, I am still very "twitter-pated". Just the thought of him makes me smile. Genesis 2:24 says, "For this reason a man will leave his father and his mother and be united to his wife, and they will become one flesh." Imagining my life without Tim was like being ripped in half.

Tim is also the teacher and godly leader of our family. His love for God and the Bible is very real. Tim definitely "practices what he preaches," and he is always studying and learning. While he was in the hospital, I yearned to trade places with him and would have in a heartbeat. Not only did I want to take his pain away, but if our children were going to have to lose a parent – I wanted it to be me. Tim has a better understanding of the Bible than anyone I know, and I couldn't stand the thought of my children losing that.

Tim is very outgoing, and he teases me by saying that I am antisocial. I'm not really. I am just a little shy and very much a homebody. I prefer staying home with my family to going out. I am a country girl that is never very comfortable in the chaos of the city. Suddenly I had to deal with phone calls, emails, visitors, doctors and nurses, and a lot of people I didn't know. I am so grateful for the many people who showed their love and support, but it was quite a change for me. At first it was tough having phone call after phone call and repeating the same updates over and over. I was fine giving out the medical updates and explaining his blood counts to everyone, but as soon as someone would say "I just know he's going to be okay", that is when I would get emotional. It was easier to deal with it on a medical level than a personal one. Soon Tim started putting his updates (whenever he was up to typing) on the website, and that made things much easier on me. There are websites out there set up to help people with this. They are extremely useful and helpful.[1] Not only did it make my load lighter by not having to explain the same updates daily, but it was nice that whoever wanted updates could get them regularly no matter where they were.

People always want to know how I handled everything. Tim says I was a rock, but I think I was Jell-O. Uneasiness seemed to be a part of every day and night. Sometimes I would wake up, see the empty pillow next to me and wonder whether Tim would ever be there again. Also, after spending a night away from the hospital, I would take a deep breath before entering his room the next day. There was always a fear of seeing an empty, clean room. Philippians 4:6-7 tells us, "Do not be anxious about anything, but in everything, by prayer and petition, with thanksgiving, present your requests to God. And the peace of God, which transcends all under-standing, will guard your hearts and your minds in Christ Jesus." Worrying doesn't change anything. Although we should not be troubled by that which we cannot change, we should try to be prepared for what might lie ahead. Sometimes we are forced to think about the unthinkable.

Besides my husband fighting for his life, other things in my life seemed to be crumbling. My great-grandmother passed away about two weeks after Tim was admitted. Two months later my grandfather suddenly and unexpectedly passed on. I chose not to go home for the funerals. That was a tough decision to make. Although I wanted to be with my family, I refused to be five hours away from Tim. If things had turned for the worse, it would have been tough to make the long drive back to Green Bay. Tim told me I could go, but being with him was my priority.

Everyday I would remind myself that God's plan is perfect and He would not give me more than I could endure (although I felt like I was at that limit). Without complete trust in God, things would have been so much harder. I often told Tim that I don't know how atheists ever endure these hardships. I cannot imagine going through tough times without knowing that God, who created everything, is in control. Colossians 1:16-17 tells us, "For by Him all things were created, things in heaven and on earth, visible and invisible, whether thrones or powers or rulers or authorities; all things were created by Him and for Him. He is before all things, and in Him all things hold together."

It also helps to have a husband that loves the Lord with all his heart. The first night in the hospital he looked at me and said, "Promise me that if I don't make it, you won't blame God." Now I had no intentions of blaming God, but Tim's greatest concern was that my faith would stay strong. I have so much respect and admiration for Tim. When tough times come, what you truly believe comes through loud and clear. Hard times test our faith. It is easy to ask "Why me?" or "How could God allow this?" and go down the path of self-pity. Or we can trust completely in God and spend more time learning His Word.

Although I am thankful to be married to a man of strong faith, I found there to be a dilemma in this. The Apostle Paul wrote, "For me, to live is Christ and to die is gain....I am torn between the two: I desire to depart and be with Christ, which is better by far..." (Philippians 1:21-23). I didn't want to be without Tim, but I also knew that being with the Lord would make Tim far happier than I ever could.

Cancer has taught me many things. Tim was put on prayer lists all over the country within days of his diagnosis. I like to say that prayer requests can move faster than cancer cells. We are so thankful for all those faithful prayer warriors. It is encouraging to know that we have a God to whom we can bring our fears and concerns. Psalms 120:1 says, "I call on the LORD in my distress, and He answers me." We may not always like the answers that we get, but we can find hope in the fact that God knows what we are going through.

I learned to appreciate the small stuff. I realize how blessed I am when Tim reaches over and takes my hand, when Tim and the kids and I are sitting around playing a board game, or when everyone is safe in bed at the end of each day.

I learned that no matter how bad things are someone always has it worse. Through this experience we met several people who were also suffering with cancer. Three people specifically, whose progress we followed, all had a worse prognosis than Tim. Two had to have surgery, and one had a bone marrow transplant. Tim, thankfully, did not need either of these procedures. All three of these people are now in remission and doing very well. Remember Job? He lost so much and suffered more than I can even imagine.

I also now have a desire to go to school for nursing. I learned how unprepared I was to take care of my family. After experiencing everything the nurses did for us, I want to be able to do that for others. We appreciated the nurses who did such a good job of caring for Tim (and me). They worked hard trying to answer all of our many questions. I found it very helpful to question everything. I wrote down daily blood counts, medications and what they did, milestones, and setbacks. Not only was it beneficial for relaying updates, but it helped me to understand everything better. Plus, I'm a big scrap-booker so of course I made a leukemia album in which my notes were handy.

I learned that it is important to listen to your body and get checked out when it is trying to tell you something. Tim knew something was not right. If he had waited longer to go in, he probably would not be here now. His platelets were so low that he was in danger of internal bleeding just sitting still. Needless to say playing basketball, wrestling with the kids, or even just falling down could have been fatal. The internet can be a great resource, but when you do not know exactly what you are looking for it can be dangerous. We checked the net to find out about the purple spots (that we now know as petechiae). The best answer we found was a heat rash which we now know was not the best answer. I still use the internet to look up health questions, but I am aware that what I read may not be accurate.

I learned that it's not over 'till it's over. This experience forced me to think about losing my husband. I had to think about what my life would be like without him. I knew that he could die, but thanks to wonderful doctors and nurses, faithful prayers from God's people, and God's awesome mercy, Tim is around to write this book.

I learned to trust completely in God's perfect plan. We would not have asked for this, nor do we want to go through it again. However, Tim has said many times that he would not trade it. We have learned a great deal, made some new friends, experienced what many others have gone through, had new opportunities, and our faith has been strengthened. Matthew 10:30 states, "And even the very hairs of your head are all numbered." This is true whether we have 100,000 hairs or 100 after chemo. I learned that God is familiar with everything we are going through, and He is involved in each situation.

Here are a few other verses that helped me during this time:

- "I can do everything through Him who gives me strength." Philippians 4:13

- "Trust in the Lord with all your heart and lean not on your own understanding; in all your ways acknowledge Him, and He will make your paths straight." Proverbs 3:5-6

- "His divine power has given us everything we need for life and godliness through our knowledge of Him who called us by His own glory and goodness." 2 Peter 1:3

- "And my God will meet all your needs according to his glorious riches in Christ Jesus." Philippians 4:19

- "God is our refuge and strength, an ever-present help in trouble." Psalm 46:1

- "No temptation has seized you except what is common to man. And God is faithful; He will not let you be tempted beyond what you can bear. But when you are tempted, He will also provide a way out so that you can stand up under it." 1 Corinthians 10:13

Appendix B:

A Physician's Perspective

By Dr. Tommy Mitchell

The Diagnosis

"You have cancer." These are the words that every patient dreads. With these words, the patient's life is changed forever. There is something about the diagnosis of a malignancy that brings on a wave of fear and uncertainty, more so than being told they have a serious infection or heart disease, even if these might be just as life threatening. The patient's world is forever changed.

Over the course of 20 years practicing medicine, I had to deliver this news to many patients. All too often, I have seen the fear in the faces of the patients and their families. I confess that after all these years, I still have not found an easy way to break the news. I sit down at the bedside, look the patient in the eye, but the Marcus Welby speech never comes. I try not to look uncomfortable, I try to be the confident professional, but somehow in the end I always seemed to stumble though the discussion. After all, these were not just names on a chart. They were very dear to me, a part of my "medical family" if you will. Most often, these were people who I had cared for over the course of many years, people who had trusted me to care for them. I remember on occasion thinking that I had somehow failed them by having to tell them they had cancer. I know this is not a realistic (or even healthy) thought process, but it was that real to me nonetheless.

Then comes the shock. An awkward few seconds, perhaps even a few tears, and then the flood of questions comes: What does this mean? How long do I have, doc? Is the treatment going to be real bad? The physician's duty at this point is to give realistic answers to these questions. The first issues are generally the operational ones, that is, those directly involving the diagnosis and treatment of the illness.

The Big Issue

After perhaps a few hours or even a day or so, the issues I had to deal with were very different. Very different and much more difficult. Now I would hear: What's going to happen to my family? Why did I get this? And, of course, why did God let this happen? Some patients were quiet and thoughtful as they considered these things. Others were loud and angry, blaming God as if He were the cause of the problem.

I often had to spend more time dealing with these questions than the questions about the treatment of the illness itself. How do you deal with the "why me" question? Well, as you have read in this book a proper understanding of the true history of the world will lead you to a correct response. We are all sinners. We are all deserving of eternal punishment. It is only through the infinite love of our Creator that we can be spared the punishment we so richly deserve.

When one is suffering it is difficult to hear that the suffering is our fault. It is certainly easier to blame someone else, most often that someone else is God. Nonetheless, truth is the truth. The truth is that we are all sinners, and we all deserve to die. So a better question might be "why do *any* of us have to die?"

God is not to blame. God is infinitely merciful, so much so that He sent His only Son to die in our place that we might have the opportunity to spend eternity with Him. In this book, Tim has very thoroughly dealt with the problem. It is only from a Christian worldview that this issue can be adequately dealt with.

It was from this perspective that I tried to counsel with my patients. We suffer because we live in a fallen and cursed world. It is not that a particular individual did something for which God is punishing them. The Bible clearly tells us:

> Luke 13:4-5 Or those eighteen who died when the tower in Siloam fell on them do you think they were more guilty than all the others living in Jerusalem? I tell you, no! But, unless you repent, you too will all perish.

So, it is not that God is punishing a particular person for something they did. Suffering is due to sin in general. Suffering is *everybody's* fault.

I had the opportunity of sharing this with my patients many times. While it did not take away the urgency of the illness, it did give many of them comfort to know that God was not punishing *them*. It also gave me the opportunity to share the Gospel with many patients and family members.

What if There's No Hope?

An unfortunate situation that existed during my years practicing medicine was that most of my medical colleagues were not Christians. I was often mocked for my beliefs. Issues of Christian morality were scoffed at. I was occasionally called names.

However, the harshest criticisms directed towards me were due to my rejection of an evolutionary worldview. Other physicians would deride me for giving up "real science" in favor of a young earth creationist belief. "How can you turn your back on the most important issue [meaning evolution] in the practice of medicine," I was asked by one of the surgeons at our local hospital.

A belief in evolution is not at all important in the practice of medicine. This has been well established in numerous articles, books, and videos, so I will not dwell on this topic here. When I challenged my friend to describe one instance in which a belief in evolution impacted the actual practice of medicine, not one example could be given.

However, I then challenged my friend to tell me how he would counsel a person facing a serious illness. "What do you say when your patients ask why they are suffering or dying?" After all, in an evolutionary scenario, death is a normal part of nature. In fact, nature cannot advance without millions and millions of organisms dying. That is what survival of the fittest requires: death, death, and more death.

Evolution requires death as a normal part of our existence. Scripture tells a very different story. 1 Corinthians 15:26 states, "The last enemy *that* shall be destroyed *is* death." Here we are clearly told that death is an enemy, an intruder that will be destroyed. If one of these positions is true, the other clearly must be false.

After pondering this for a moment, my friend replied, "I guess I would just tell them, 'That's just the way it is.'" I could not help but wonder how little comfort that might be to a desperately ill person. I know that my colleague was a caring physician, and he wanted to do his very best for every patient. I did not (nor do I to this day) question that he had compassion. He merely could not justify his compassion given his unbiblical foundation. What a pity.

Conclusion

In the countless times I counseled sick and dying patients, I was thankful that the Lord was with me. I pray that the patients heard His words and not mine during their most difficult trials. The problems regarding the "hows" of sickness (How do we test for it? How do we treat it?) were much less important than the "whys" of sickness (Why is this happening to me? Why did God allow this?). The "hows" were temporal, the "whys" were eternal.

I am thankful that Tim was led to share the trials of his illness with us all. This book will, I pray, be helpful not only to those facing a personal or family illness. Tim's experiences should be a wake-up call for the Church to recognize how important this issue is to our society at the present time. It is only through an understanding of the true history of the world that we can truly have an answer to this question.

Glossary of Medical Terms

(All definitions are based on Wikipedia's definitions,
unless otherwise noted.)

Acute Promyelocytic Leukemia – this is the type of leukemia that I had. It is also called APL or M3 for short and is a type of acute myeloid leukemia (AML).

Anemia – a qualitative or quantitative deficiency of hemoglobin, a molecule found inside red blood cells

ATRA – stands for All-Trans Retinoic Acid and is also called Vesanoid. This is the wonder drug for my type of leukemia. It works by forcing the immature cancerous cells to mature and die.

CT scan – a medical imaging method which generates a three-dimensional image of the inside of an object, such as a person.

Disseminated Introvascular Coagulation (DIC) – a pathological process in the body where the blood starts to coagulate throughout the whole body. This depletes the body of its platelets and coagulation factors, and there is a paradoxically increased risk of hemorrhage. It occurs in critically ill patients, especially those with...acute promyelocytic leukemia.

Electrocardiogram – **(EKG)** a graph which records the electrical activity of the heart over time. It is used to indicate the overall rhythm of the heart, and weaknesses in different parts of the heart muscle.

Esophagogastroduodenoscopy – **(EGD)** a procedure that visualizes the upper part of the gastrointestinal tract up to the duodenum

Idarubacin – the type of chemotherapy treatment that I received for my first, second, and fourth rounds.

Mitoxantrone – the type of chemotherapy treatment that I received for my third round.

MUGA scan – a test to evaluate the function of the heart ventricles. Radioactive technetium is injected into the bloodstream so that it can be observed as it is circulated through the heart.

Neutropenia – a blood disorder characterized by an abnormally low number of neutraphil granulocytes (a type of white blood cell).

Neutrophil – most abundant and mature type of white blood cell and form an essential part of the immune system.

Oncologist – a physician who studies, diagnoses, and treats various forms of cancer.

Petechiae – pinpoint flat round red spots under the skin surface caused by intradermal hemorrhage (bleeding into the skin). Petechiae are red because they contain red blood that has leaked from the capillaries into the skin.

PICC Line - stands for Peripherally Inserted Central Catheter. They are used to administer medicines and fluids to the body. My particular PICC line ran from the inside of my upper left arm into a main blood vessel a couple of inches from my heart.

Platelet – (also known as thrombocytes) are tiny cells in the bloodstream that are vital to the clotting process. Normal platelet counts should be between 140 – 440 and mine were under 20 when I checked in.

Thrombocytopenia - According to the NetDoctor website, "Thrombocytopenia is the term for a reduced platelet (thrombocyte) count. It happens when platelets are lost from the circulation faster than they can be replaced from the bone marrow where they are made."

White Blood Cell (WBC) – cells of the immune system defending the body against both infectious disease and foreign materials.

Endnotes:

Introduction:

1 See *Old Earth Creationism on Trial* by Tim Chaffey and Dr. Jason Lisle (Green Forest, AR: Master Books, 2008).

Chapter 1:

1 Midwest Apologetics is the name of the ministry founded and directed by the author. For more information, please see the website at: <www.midwestapologetics.org>.

2 The original journal can still be viewed at: <www.midwestapologetics.org/leukemia.htm>.

3 It is possible that her comments were meant for good. Perhaps she saw his painful and pitiful state and thought he could end it all by dying and going to be with God.

Chapter 3:

1 We are not sure who wrote the Book of Hebrews. Some scholars believe it was Paul. If so, then Paul would have written fourteen books.

Chapter 4:

1 Six months after this event, I was given an opportunity to share my testimony contained in this book at a conference in Green Bay. As it turned out, the man that wheeled me to the ear, nose, throat specialist

was in attendance during that talk, as was one of my regular nurses. It was a blessing to be able to say "thank you" to both of these people.

2   The information for Spafford's story comes from *Then Sings My Soul* by Robert J. Morgan (Nashville, TN: Thomas Nelson, 2003), 185.

Chapter 6:

1   For more on this amazing father-son team, see their website at: <www. teamhoyt.com>.

2   This term is used on the Hoyt's website.

Chapter 8:

1   This subject was handled at length in my previous book with Dr. Jason Lisle. The Big Bang has been challenged by both Christian and secular scientists so the objections are not merely religious in nature.

2   This is known as the problem of infinite regress.

3   Some physicists have sought an answer to this issue in the field of quantum physics. They claim that subatomic particles seem to be capable of popping in and out of existence. They then reason that perhaps our universe popped into existence from one of these quantum fluctuations. However, this is illogical because it is comparing apples to oranges. Even if particles in our universe today can go in and out of existence, it must be kept in mind that they are doing this in an already existing universe. This cannot be equated with an entire universe, or the singularity from which our universe allegedly sprang, popping into existence from nothing.

4   The various forms of the Cosmological Argument have been explained in detail by many Christian scholars. It is beyond the scope of this book to rehash all of the details here. My point is to reveal what these arguments tell us about God.

5   The Intelligent Design Movement's strengths and weaknesses were dealt with in my first book, *Old Earth Creationism on Trial*. Although it has some strengths, I would advise Christians to be wary of the Intelligent Design Movement. A few of my reasons for this will be discussed in this section.

6   The New Testament repeats nine of the Ten Commandments in one form or another. The only one that is not restated is the Sabbath Day commandment. Paul told the Colossians that no one should judge them concerning the Sabbath Day (Col. 2:16). Nevertheless, the principle that God requires our time and devotion still stands.

7 Please understand that I was not saying these things as prideful boasts. They were calculated statements to illustrate the absurdity of his argument.

8 C.S. Lewis, *Mere Christianity*, 45-46.

9 Immanence refers to God's closeness to His creation. Although He is not part of the creation, as in pantheism, He is everywhere present and can step into His creation and act whenever, wherever, and however He wills.

Chapter 9:

1 Although it differs from Buddhism in other aspects, the belief system known as Christian Science says essentially the same thing on this point – that pain and suffering are illusory. As such, it fails at the same point as Buddhism on this subject, and should not ever be confused with biblical Christianity.

2 The fact that Mormons often try to lead Christians to convert to Mormonism demonstrates that they do not really view themselves as another Christian denomination. They believe they represent the true church and all others that call themselves Christians are following churches that have gone astray.

Chapter 10:

1 Genesis 3:14 indicates that the serpent was cursed "more than" all the other animals. We can conclude that the rest of the animals were cursed – just not to the same degree as the serpent.

2 It is beyond the scope of this book to deal with the concepts of free will and predestination. It is my belief that a person does not have to pick one or the other because they can both be held to be true. I believe God predestines all that happens but does not negate man's will in the process. There are many faithful Christians who would not agree with my conclusions on this particular issue.

3 This issue was covered in great detail in my first book, *Old-Earth Creationism on Trial*, co-authored with Dr. Jason Lisle.

4 If God did not agree with Jesus' message, then it is hard to see why He would have raised Him from the dead, since He would then appear to be endorsing the message of a false prophet.

Appendix A:

1 See <www.carepages.com> for one example. This site was very helpful for us to keep track of a few other people we know who have suffered through a cancer battle.

About the Author

Tim lives with his wife and two children in Southern Wisconsin. He is currently serving as an Associate Pastor and has taught high school Bible and Science classes for six years.

Tim is the founder and director of Midwest Apologetics, a ministry dedicated to defending God's Word from beginning to end. He holds a Bachelors and a Masters degree in Biblical and Theological Studies, as well as a Master of Divinity, specializing in Apologetics and Theology. He is currently working on a Ph.D. in Apologetics and Theology from Liberty Baptist Theological Seminary.

He co-authored *Old-Earth Creationism on Trial* with astrophysicist, Jason Lisle, Ph.D. He has also written *God Means What He Says: A Biblical Critique of the Framework Hypothesis*. Tim is currently working on an exciting youth fiction series (tentatively titled *The Truth Chronicles*), which has an apologetic focus, and deals with many of the issues young people face today. The first two books in the series should be published in 2009.

Tim also speaks on a variety of topics related to apologetics. For a full list of titles, booking information, and much more, visit <www.midwestapologetics.org> or <midwest apologetics.blogspot.com>.

Printed in the United States
139610LV00001BB/2/P